Creative Supervision

Creative Supervision

The Use of Expressive Arts Methods in Supervision and Self-supervision

Mooli Lahad

Jessica Kingsley Publishers
London and Philadelphia

First published in the United Kingdom in 2000
by Jessica Kingsley Publishers
116 Pentonville Road
London N1 9JB, UK
and
400 Market Street, Suite 400
Philadelphia, PA 19106, USA

www.jkp.com

Copyright © Mooli Lahad 2000
Printed digitally since 2010

Library of Congress Cataloging in Publication Data
Lahad, Mooli,
    Creative supervision : the use of expressive arts methods in supervision
and self-supervision / Mooli Lahad.
        p.   cm.
    ISBN 1 85302 828 2 (alk. paper)
    1. Psychotherapists--Supervision of. 2. Arts--Therapeutic use.
    I. Title.
    RC459.1.34   1999   99-41623
    616.89'14--dc21   CIP

British Library Cataloguing in Publication Data
Lahad, Mooli
    Creative supervision : the use of expressive arts methods in
    supervision and self-supervision
    1. Arts - Therapeutic use 2. Psychotherapists
    1. Title
    616.8'9165

ISBN 978 1 85302 828 1

Contents

Preface

Let's start at the very beginning. After all, as Maria in *The Sound of Music* suggested, 'It is a very good place to start.' My beginning is a Hassidic story that I have heard being transformed and changed over the years.

A long time ago there was an old rabbi who loved to teach. He had taught for so many generations that he could hardly remember them all. This old rabbi enjoyed teaching the alphabet to little children, but he was actually famous for one thing, he was known as a mindreader. Everyone believed in his powers and no one ever doubted them.

One day, when the man was very old, a child named Moishe decided to challenge him. Moishe began to think of a way to disprove the rabbi's powers. He thought and thought, pacing back and forth until his feet carved a path in the ground. Finally, he had an idea. He would go to the field and catch a butterfly. Then, holding it in his hands, he would run to the old man and ask him, 'Rabbi, what do I have in my hand?' He was quite sure that the rabbi would say 'a butterfly'. He would ask the rabbi, 'Is it alive or dead?' If the rabbi said it was dead, then Moishe would open his hand and let the butterfly fly away. But if he said it was alive, he would squeeze the butterfly between his hands and show the dead butterfly to the rabbi.

With this brilliant idea he ran to the field to catch a butterfly. Sure enough, when you look for something and you really want to find it, you will succeed. And so in no time at all, Moishe had a butterfly in his hands, and breathlessly ran to the rabbi.

The old man was sleepy when Moishe came into the room. The boy held the butterfly in his hands, tried not to squeeze it, nor to giggle as it tickled his hands, and asked the first question. 'Rabbi, what do I have in my hands?' The old man began to think and after a while said, 'A butterfly, my son, a butterfly.' Moishe was pleased and with shining eyes he asked, 'Is it alive or dead?' The old man closed his eyes and stroked his long, white beard. This time he thought for a long time. When at last he opened

his eyes he said in a soft voice, 'It's all in your hands, my son, it is all in your hands...'

This book is not about mindreading. Rather, it is about mutual respect and the reciprocal process. It is about finding the many results that joint efforts can produce. Almost like the rabbi's exclamation 'It's all in your hands...'. More than anything else, it is in the hands of all partners, or counterparts as I like to call them, to find the best way forward.

Therefore this book is not exclusively for supervisors and their supervisees, nor is it limited to work with individuals or groups. Indeed it can be used as a tool in and of itself for professional or peer supervision or in any other creative situations for which it could be useful.

My personal suggestion is to use this book gently, keeping in mind the boundaries of others as well as yourself and allowing your own supportive nature, warmth and playfulness to be present.

Perhaps other things should be said: Believe in what you hear; listen as a four-year-old child listens; open your heart, eyes, and ears to nuances and to silence; and be patient; try to avoid interpretation; ask open-ended questions, which imply interest in others; do not criticize.

As you may already see, I have chosen to write this book as a dialog. Dialog is what I believe supervision, as well as therapy, is all about. I have also tackled the troublesome grammatical question of gender, the way I have in my lectures for the past 20 years: by writing some parts in the female and some in the male gender. I do not like the current 's/he' solution that looks and sounds like a registration form, nor do I like 'the person' solution. We were created as male and female and that combination means LIFE. So please bear with my awkward solution.

This book is first and foremost dedicated to my beloved wife Vered, who taught me about joy, playfulness, smiling, and crying. She takes care of our four lovely children whenever I travel around the globe; first studying, then teaching. It is quite easy to travel far when you know that the home is secure and well taken care of. My children Tom, Michal, Omri, and Ofer were, and still are, my companions in so many nights of storytelling and singing. My mother, Naomi, truly taught me what it means to care and to love unconditionally. My sister Shlomit, is a unique combination of affection, wisdom, and the supernatural; she taught me to trust nature and the importance of knowing the self.

Thanks to my many colleagues and students who agreed to experiment with these methods, and whose reactions, remarks, and suggestions are very much a part of this book.[1] Special thanks go also to my three very special teachers and friends whose 'fingerprints' can be found all over this book: Dr Ofra Ayalon, Professor Sue Emmy Jennings, and Dr Violet Oaklander.

Reference will be made in this book only to those exercises I have specifically quoted or adapted from others. At the same time one must remember that over these 20 years of supervision I have developed my own techniques, my own versions of other techniques, and all sorts of combinations. Let me take this opportunity to thank the many minds from whom I absorbed knowledge and ideas. I apologize for not always remembering where it all started. For it all probably started 'in the beginning'. Let me reassure my reader that I will be pleased, in years to come, to belong to those before me and only mentioned as an inspiration.

---

[1]   Thank you to Michal Sasson for her wonderful photography.

Introduction

Ankori (1989), in his book about myths and the Western world, suggests that the Western world divorced itself from the world of fantasy some centuries ago, when it found science and married itself to logic and realistic thinking.

Although much more accepted today, the world of lateral thinking, the world of experiencing and feeling, the world of imagination and fantasy, and the world of the supernatural have always been treated as second or third best. Even for the revolutionary movement of psychoanalysis that delves into the world of free association and dreams, fantasy is not the desired outcome. It is merely a tool for psychoanalysts to understand and to analyze.

In our modern world where industry and technology seek new ideas, creativity is perceived as a tool to sell products. This is a fair approach. Let's pretend for a moment, however, that you are choosing between two employment applicants. The report from the first interview says, 'Looks honest, clever, uses fantasy and imagination, is very creative, sometimes spaces out.' The second report says, 'Looks honest, clever, uses grounded and logical thinking, creative yet critical and sophisticated.' Which applicant would you choose for the job? My best guess is the second.

However, denigration of the imagination does not begin with job seeking. Rather, it starts during the early school days. Let us look at the main demands in primary school. Which child succeeds? The child with imagination, creativity and fantasies? Or the cognitive, logical and rational, thinking child? How do teachers describe the first type of child? In Israel they call them astronauts; in other places, they are termed overimaginative, spaced out and introverted. The latter type of child will be described by teachers as being clever, clear, logical, rational, with a problem-solving mind.

Once we grow up we are told that in order to solve problems you need to use your imagination and be creative. How is this done? We have criticized these mental processes for so long that we are unsure how to retrieve them. For so long we are told to stop dreaming, to think practically, to show evidence, and to prove everything. When we finally become therapists, we are told that intuition is not enough. We must justify and quantify. When, under supervision, you share your fantasies, dreams, and images, they are mostly used to help you learn about your countertransference.

If you disclose, for example, that you are repelled by your client's odors, or by his gestures or smelly breath, it is assumed that these are important issues for personal therapy, or for working on countertransference, or 'unfinished business'. But almost *never* are these reactions considered as an important piece of information coming from the right hemisphere of your brain, your non-logical thinking or your circular rather than linear perception.

We, belonging to Western society, are so afraid of these processes that we claim that children do not know how to differentiate between imagination and reality. By inference, this means that adults not only can make the differentiation but must make it. The question remains, are children really unable to differentiate? Maybe they are still able to move between reality and fantasy without fear, without the critical approach that one is better than the other. Maybe they believe that it is safe to get lost in a fantasy land without hesitation. We know that even a writer who writes about the land of fantasy warns us of its hazards. As profoundly put by Ande (undated), *The Never Ending Story* warns us of getting lost in fantasy and how dangerous it is. To illustrate it he uses two colors in his book: one for when it is 'reality' and another when it is 'fantasy', as if to make sure that the reader won't get lost. One should wonder, isn't a story a fiction any way?

My argument is that children *can* differentiate between fantasy and reality. They know that they can turn a chair into a horse and fight a battle. They know if the horse is galloping or stopping, eating or hungry. But when a parent enters the room and suggests that the horse is trotting or asks if we shall give him some food, the child will rather quickly respond, 'Oh Daddy, it is just a chair.' On other occasions the child will ask the parent to leave the room while playing imaginative games.

So what has happened? Where and when do we lose this ability? Why are we so perplexed in the face of imagination? Why are we so defensive and apologetic in supervision when we share our non-logical thinking, circular perception, images, smells, inner pictures, metaphors, and lateral thinking? Is it because we find them hard to defend? Are we afraid of hearing that it is countertransference? Or is it a forgotten language, and is Fantasyland a feared place?

Let me share another observation: the contrast between the 'fixed price/no fantasy' selling of Western traders, and the 'bargaining/story time' approach of the Arab market. Let's observe the dialog in the Arab market. First they check: how are you? Then they talk about the news and tell stories, then there is the to and fro of price negotiation, drinking coffee, another story and price bargaining; and then at the end, the deal is on, both salesperson and customer are satiated like after a very nutritious meal. And if there is no bargain, so what? At least they have good stories to tell.

What a waste of time…because in Western eyes TIME IS MONEY. Are they such less successful merchants? I doubt it, yet they are more satisfied at the end of the day; not only have they sold something, but also they made human contact and heard a story.

We have lost it all, we go into these huge malls where all the prices are fixed, the salesperson is anonymous and we consume without any price negotiation – till where a dehumanized person is passing the merchandise like the actors in the Charlie Chaplin film *Modern Times*. We go out of the shops hungry although we think we are satiated, only to come back the next day to consume again. We have lost our ability to tell stories in our daily life; we buy and buy, but with no story there is no real connection and communication. And that is for me why we buy so many unnecessary things till the next time we raid the supermarket.

This book is about using the right hemisphere and the analogical dreamlike mechanisms in the service of UNDERSTANDING the processes of therapy, intervention and support. It is a book about helping therapists to get in touch with the other 50 per cent of their experience, and that of the client's, in order to get out of loopholes, pitfalls, and resistance. It will allow therapists to see alternatives and the value of experiencing other senses, and thus to be able to make sense of situations for themselves as well as for their clients.

This book is not about divorcing the left hemisphere of the brain from the right. It is about reintroducing the left side of our brain to the right side in order to make them equal partners (and maybe friends) in the effort to become a better, more whole person who is able to communicate more flexibly with a multidimensional use of self and others. Hence, I will introduce various techniques that I have used in the last 20 years as a supervisor in trying to build a bridge between creativity, fantasy, and logic.

'Supervision' comprises two words: 'super' and 'vision'. Bernard and Goodyear (1993) suggest that one of the main skills of the supervisor is the ability to have this view over a range of perspectives in order to assist in understanding and evaluating a situation. Kadushin's (1992) approach to supervision is integrative. He defines three aspects of supervision: administrative, educational, and supportive. Hawkins and Shohat (1989) describe the supervision process as one that is intended to level up the personal and vocational skills of the supervisee.

Supervision of arts therapists intends to do just this, but most of it is carried out in an adapted 'language'. This is to say that, in many cases, supervision of arts and dramatherapists is conducted using psychological language and concepts. It is very important for dramatherapy as a profession to develop its own language, theories, set of concepts, and 'supervision' language. This does not imply alienation from the world of psychology and psychotherapy, but rather that these languages should be incorporated into dramatherapy as an arts profession.

In spite of the reports existing in the literature about combining metaphors and stories in the therapeutic process, there is practically no reference made to tools and techniques from this area of supervision. Ekstein and Wallerstein (1972) distinguish between three directions in supervision:

1.   Patient-centered supervision

2.   Therapist-centered supervision

3.   Process-centered supervision.

Supervisor and supervisee can deal with theories, techniques and diagnosis, and can decide together upon a line of treatment giving the supervision session a consultative tone. They can deal with the feelings and requests of the supervisee and give the supervision session a more treatment-oriented tone. Furthermore, they can deal with any ongoing interactions and focus the supervision on interpersonal and other parallel processes.

Many times in supervision, after deciding on the direction and desired content, I find myself debating a further dilemma: Should I stay within the realms of thought and logic (left hemisphere of the brain) or should I expand to the realms of imagination and experience (right hemisphere of the brain) and develop the dialog between the two realms? As a therapist, this extension is quite acceptable to me and I find it to be greatly beneficial. This generalization into the area of supervision demands additional thought. This book works with many examples to illustrate these extensions. It is important to stress that the use of metaphors, images, and stories is not offered as a substitute for other methods of supervision; they do not come in place of theoretical understanding and do not prevent the defining of therapeutic aims, but provide different ways of looking at things.

The styles of work that I describe are likely to help in many supervision situations, from making a diagnosis and deciding upon a therapeutic approach to understanding the therapeutic process and the therapist–client relationships. I have found this particularly suitable in situations where the supervisee is 'stuck', or where there is resistance or a tendency to rationalize. In these types of situations, this approach can be used to empower people to cope with difficulties by strengthening introspection and the visualization of concepts and problems. It introduces the experiential-emotional approaches to supervisees who tend to intellectualize through finding latent internal creative resources. It also strengthens the supervisee's feeling of resourcefulness; and through it they find a new sense of control.

The use of metaphors, stories, images, and similar expressive media, whether in the therapeutic or in the supervision process, is based on the assumption that a story or image can represent the objective or subjective perception of internal or external reality. Relating to the representative image is likely to change internal reality, or can bring about a change in perceiving the external reality, but it does not aspire to achieve change in the objective reality itself. For example, when a supervisee uses an image of a locomotive for a client it is not only a metaphor of being a driving force or bulling, but various questions can be explored: Is there a driver? How old is he? How old is the locomotive? Is he at a junction? And so on. Now this metaphoric exploration, as it will be illustrated many times in the book, is opening options but does not change reality.

If supervisor and supervisee agree to work with metaphors, then the supervisee needs to understand how the process works. The 'rules of the game' and teaching the metaphoric way of thinking can help the supervisee understand the concept of the 'quest' or journey of the hero as a way of understanding the psyche's encounter with the world and its quest for maturation. Locating the 'great story' and transcending into the fantastic reality where time and space are suspended, and where the impossible is made possible, can help the supervisee to observe a situation from new perspectives and broaden alternatives. The supervisee is more able to devise ways of preventing something from happening and enabling the transition from a current situation to a desired one.

During the supervision session, it is possible to stay within the realm of images and metaphor, and not to concern oneself with explanations and interpretations. Staying *with* the metaphor is different from using metaphors as unconscious material to be brought into consciousness. Supervisors and supervisees who are involved can find the real counterparts and 'translate' the language of images into the language of reality, when appropriate.

CHAPTER I

Starting Your Supervision

It is not so easy to start supervision with supervisees who have already been to several supervisors in the past, most of whom are 'talking left brain supervision'. They come for your supervision but they expect to get the same outcome or, as Minuchin (1974) describes it, to dance the same dance.

First we need to get to know each other, just as the fox told the Little Prince (de Saint-Exupéry 1982): "'You must be very patient," replied the fox. "First you will sit down at a little distance from me... I shall look at you...and you will say nothing... But you will sit a little closer to me, every day..."' (p.65.) Later the fox talks about the importance of rituals. "'One must observe the proper rites..." said the fox. "What is a rite?" asked the little prince. "They are what make one day different from other days..."' (p.66.) So we are in supervision observing rites.

However, we need to specify both our contract and our rituals. One very important thing for me is that *I am at the service of my supervisee*. This means that we will rarely do anything that does not respond to her needs or that is not in our agreed contract.

We will usually use 'client-centered' supervision where the client's needs and well-being are the focus of our engagement. This is not to say that we will avoid what is going on for the therapist-supervisee in this encounter, but most often her private life will not be the focus of our meeting. If, however, personal issues do come up and we feel they are appropriate for us to deal with, they will be brought out in the open. Or, we can discuss whether it is best for the supervisee to seek help from her own therapist. At times it is the supervisor's feelings or 'counter-transference' that may come up. And when that happens I usually bring it as a question rather than a statement checking whether it makes any sense to the supervisee.

I remember not long ago when I was leading a group supervision and Rania, one supervisee, told us that she was working with unemployed men and women. She brought to them the story of the Wizard of Oz. She continually talked about how she tried to force them to see that there was no wizard and that it was 'all in their hands'. I suddenly was so frustrated and said, 'But can't you see how difficult it is for them to give up the dream? For Dorothy and her friends it is a process, a journey not an immediate outcome.' Rania was shocked; she had never experienced such intervention from me, she was paralyzed and felt that I had offended her. Was it not that I was doing to Rania what she did to her group? Definitely so.

So I accepted responsibility and shared how much more protective I felt toward her group and less of her. (In my own supervision I then realized that it was connected to my own experience with my late father who was made redundant many years ago in a very humiliating act, and so I reacted not only for that group of unemployed people, but also on my own personal unfinished business with unemployment.) The very interesting outcome of this supervision session was a process of deeper understanding of the story the Wizard of Oz, and its connection to our lives, specially to Rania's difficulty to admit her inner voices as Dorothy's oppressing aunt. Then again when we looked into the story we realized that only through Dorothy's journey can she learn to give up fantasy and realize that it is the real personal effort that we made that gets us in touch with our inner 'wizard', which is in a way also the aunt's voice.

A very important part of this encounter is the fact that we are dealing with metaphor, images, and fantasy. As I mentioned earlier, they are rather difficult to access for many people, both because they have been suppressed and criticized and because people are afraid of what will come out. What will I disclose? Or rather, what will my unconscious reveal about me? So many of these fears and critical thoughts are put into our brains that it will take time until the supervisee can use a crayon freely or fantasize openly. Most will surely enjoy the odd session of relaxation combined with guided imagery or visualization, but not everyone will be ready to share their fantasies or images with the supervisor or colleagues.

I must comment that the Jungian therapists and supervisors are somewhat different in so far as they do use images, myth, and fantasy. However, the outcome of the process is like regular Jungian interpretative therapy, rather than as a client-centered approach. *We need to remember that in order to be able to use the right hemisphere of the brain in a free and friendly way, we need to train the mind to become flexible in using it.*

Sometimes I start by telling the story of how we were taught to forget about that side of the brain early in our schooldays, describing the hardships of the imaginative child who is so often called an 'astronaut'. An 'astronaut' is a very special child who sees things in different ways and from different perspectives, in images rather than in sequence. This child understands very quickly the structure of the normal lesson where the teacher usually has to repeat everything at least three times for the other students. After a while, she learns to 'space out' to her 'spacecraft', to think on her own and to imagine things that are somewhat connected, and later on more remotely connected, to the lesson. Whenever she 'lands', she understands what is being taught, but unfortunately she doesn't land in the right place, in sequence of the three repetitions. She may well land at sequence five, seven, or nine. Therefore, she is not always 'with the class'.

What is also very interesting is that there are times when only the imaginative child responds to the teacher's question. Suddenly, seemingly out of the blue, the teacher asks a 'circular' *Weltanschauung* question. No one really dares to answer, or maybe no one really understands, what the teacher is asking. The question involves the use of imagination relating to aspects of the lesson that are not directly connected to what has been explained. The imaginative child puts up her hand and…yes, she gets it right. The teacher is astonished and writes in her notebook, 'flash of brilliance'.

Perhaps a good example can come from the following joke I used to tell teachers: 'Sara, an experienced teacher is waiting outside a supermarket on a rainy day with two heavy bags. She is soaking wet and there are no taxis available. Suddenly a beautiful big Bentley stops near her and the driver invites her in. She sits in the back seat and the man asks her, "Hey teacher, do you remember me?" She looks puzzled and says, "Sorry, no." "I am Steve and all that I have today, this car and my business, is thanks to you." Sara looks amazed and Steve continues, "You see, teacher, you remember you taught us math?", "Yes," she nods her head. "And you remember teaching us percentages?" "Yes," she nods again. "So, you see teacher, I buy for $1.00 and sell for $100.00 – 10 per cent profit is enough for me, isn't it?"'

In my 20 years of school psychology I could trace these children easily. When sitting in the class I used to see a pattern that happened quite often when the imaginative child raised his hand. The teachers, knowing that the child's question would be rather difficult to handle, and that it might confuse the other students, would often say, 'Not now, Dory.' Soon the Dorys learn that now will never come, and so develop the spacecraft technique.

As another way of starting supervision, I tell the story of the survival of people in extreme situations who use their fantasy space as an escape – or, as I usually refer to it, 'transcend into fantastic reality'. I tell them about the two brothers who, during the Holocaust, lost their parents and had to run from one hiding place to another. These boys, one of whom is a famous Israeli writer Uri Orlev, played an imaginative game with one another before the war. They had heard that a long time ago there was a dynasty in China ruled by Mandarins. As young children they thought the name was given because these kings and princes had mandarins on their heads. This story made the boys laugh. When the war started and they had to run from place to place, the older brother (the writer Orlev) made up a story for them. He told his younger brother: 'We are the sons of the Emperor of China and we are Mandarins. Our father commanded us to dream a dream about war.' He made an agreement with his little brother that whenever they clenched their fists and said 'Mandarin' they would revert to their dream of war.

As hard as it is to believe, these two orphans came through many instances of direct threats to their lives by using the technique of transcendence into fantastic reality. To describe this technique, some may use the terms dissociation and denial; but in my mind, these terms only serve as defensive, rejecting, and non-observant points of view. There are many more examples of the vital role of the imagination in the saving of lives. Therefore, the use of these clinical diagnostic terms is often not really helpful in understanding the power of this phenomenon. Instead, let us explore the phenomenon of transcendence into fantastic reality.

One way to make contact with the fantastic reality is the following exercise. You may try it with your eyes open or closed.

Sit in a comfortable position, without making any special effort. Give yourself feedback on where you are. Do you feel the chair you are sitting on? Do you feel where your hands are? Do they touch anything: each other, a piece of cloth, an object? Where are your legs? On the floor, one on top of the other, stretched, on your heels? Do you feel any tension? You may change the way you sit at any time. Can you hear your breathing? Do not make any effort, just listen to it. Pay attention to the fact that when the air goes in, you can feel it, and when it goes out, it disappears. Now, try and take a deep breath…and another one. This is good.

Try to feel the difference in your eyes while your eyelids are slowly closing. See the reduction of light shining into the eyes until the eyelids are closed. You may slowly open them again, just to sense the difference, and then close them slowly again. Or you may decide to keep your eyes open.

Listen to your breathing, listen to your heartbeat, and try to take another deep breath. Now, as you sit here, please go inside yourself. Try to listen to your third ear, the ear we use in order to listen inside ourselves. Please try to hear your name called out in the way you like most. Listen to the sounds of a voice calling out your name in the most pleasant, warm, reassuring, and loving way you like to hear it. It may be a nickname, or a name not used for a long time. It can be a name from the past, the present or the way you would like it to be in the future.

Let the sound come to you. You may experience a quarrel between several sounds coming up at the same time. You may hear some unpleasant sounds. Say goodbye to them now.

You may find that you need more time to find the sound that you want to concentrate on. Take your time. When you find that sound, breathe deeply and just let it resonate in your body... Now try to see what are the images, colors, or shapes that come to mind. It may be of the rhythm or of the sensation or the feelings. *Believe* in what you see.

Soon I'll ask you to open your eyes, to take crayons and paper, and to draw on a piece of paper the images of the meeting with the sounds of your name you like the most.

On 'coming back', I ask my supervisee to share as much as she wants about the process. Many talk about warmth, love, and caring memories, together with the longing for that sound and the pain of it, now that it has gone. We talk about the importance of loving and caring voices in our lives, but more so about the experience they had in the fantastic reality. They could sometimes hear the voice, or even see the person or the situation in which this voice was heard and how vivid it sounded.

For many of my supervisees this is a confirmation of their ability to get in touch with the experiences of the fantastic reality, but also how easy it is to get strength and self-nurturing from this part of ourselves. Many take this experience as a simple self-relaxation, self-nurturing exercise and some go back home, asking the real owner of that sound to reproduce it more often so that they can feel it in reality.

As a rule we discuss the techniques that we will use. These will not exclude straightforward talking. We will always move back and forth between reality (left-brain functions) and fantastic reality (right-brain functions). We agree that the supervisee can bring in what ever feels right: a song, a poem, a picture, or any item that she feels can help us to understand the process. In my supervision group, which can at times be for five hours, I add that sometimes we will have the supervision sessions outside, in nature. Unfortunately we don't do this enough, even less so with individuals. I often find the practicalities of going out to be rather difficult, mainly due to the time constraints of the session.

I also tell my supervisee that we will be using art materials such as crayons, Plasticine, and clay. We will use therapeutic cards, stories, fairy tales, films, metaphors, and any other method that can help. We will use drama, theater 'directions' and psychodramatic exercises, free writing and small world (that is using small objects, dolls and other small artefacts such as coins, buttons, or pebbles). These are all techniques to get a fresh and different perspective on things.

The use of interpretation will be almost nil, unless requested by the supervisee. Most of the time, introspection and lateral reflection are encouraged as a way to jointly investigate the 'product'. At times, we also use the gestalt approach of exploration and listening, such as personifying an object and letting it explore itself, its surroundings, etc. This is how we usually start our journey into creative explorations.

Colors, Shapes, and Lines

What is so fishy about Judy?

Gabriela is a very experienced social worker. She has worked for a long time with very difficult cases, most of which deal with domestic violence and abuse. She comes to supervision every fortnight, and we usually find it very helpful to discuss her caseload with metaphors and images.

One time, she came in very upset. She was dealing with a teenage girl, Judy, who was being raised by a single mother who continuously calls Gabriela for advice and help, but rarely uses her advice. Gabriela had never brought Judy's case to supervision before. This time, however, she was determined to understand what was going wrong with Judy.

The story of Judy was rather usual to many teenagers of her background. She emigrated from Russia to Israel with her mother and grandmother in 1991. (Her father stayed in Russia, as in fact he had been living with another woman for some time.) They got an apartment and shared it with another single-parent family for three years. Not long after they arrived in Israel, Judy's grandmother died. Her mother dated on-and-off, until about a year ago when she married B, himself a Russian immigrant, unemployed for a long time. The school counselor for truancy suspected that the adults and possibly even Judy abused drugs.

Judy had many behavioral problems, which is why she was referred to Gabriela. She was diagnosed with high intelligence, low self-esteem and some signs of learning disabilities. For about five months Gabriela saw Judy, and every so often, her mother. Judy described her mother to Gabriela as a childish person, constantly seeking men's attention, and wishing Judy to disappear from her life.

Gabriela tried several different methods – counseling the mother alone, counseling the mother and daughter together, she even made a home visit. Eventually, Gabriela reached a point where she felt that it was all right to see Judy alone. It was okay to see her mum alone, but it was a disaster when she saw them together, and in their home it was even worse. Last week when the school counselor called Gabriela to tell her that Judy was found on the beach with a man suspected of drug dealing, Gabriela was at a loss.

After a long discussion, I suggested to Gabriela to do the following 'Colors, Shapes, and Lines' exercise. I asked her to pick from the crayons one color for Judy, one for Judy's mum, one for the mother's new man, and one for herself. Then I asked her to take a piece of paper and paint these colors in any shapes or lines she wanted. Gabriela's image for Judy's family and for herself in it is shown in Figure 2.1. Once she finished drawing, I asked for her reactions to it. She responded, 'Clearly, it is a mess.'

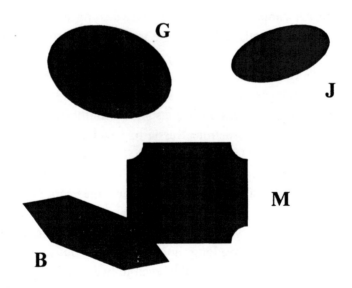

G = Gabriela
M = Mother
J = Judy
B = Mother's husband

Figure 2.1 What's so fishy about Judy?

	Judy	Mum	B	Gabriela
			Table 2.1 Gabriela's chart of Judy's family		
Color	blue	dark brown	bright red	purple
First association	sea in summer	blood	torero	queen
Other ideas	winter, sky, cold, ice	shit, mud, soil, dry	sun, happy, hot, fire	lily, stone, rich
Tempo	wavy	slow	swift	gentle
Weight	heavy	very heavy	light	medium
Animal	fish	shark	lion	snail
Season	winter	desert	summer storm	spring evening
Clothing	swimsuit	boots	dancing shoes	party dress
Scenery	sea	desert	sunset	evening

I then asked for Gabriela's permission to give my observations on the image she drew. I pointed out the fact that, in the picture, Judy is far from her mother and closer to her; that the mother is between Judy and Gabriela. That the mother's 'thorns' are toward Gabriela and gentle curves toward Judy. That the mother is so close to B that he covers the edges of her shape. Regarding the use of color, I pointed out to Gabriela that mother (dark brown) and B (bright red) were darker colors of the 'warm family'; Judy (blue) of the 'cold family'; and herself, Gabriela, a mixed color – purple (blue and red). I then had Gabriela fill in a color chart. The results of this are very interesting (Table 2.1).

We first looked at the chart vertically, and I asked her whether anything was in agreement with her ideas; or did it still look surprising or impossible. Gabriela looked at Judy's list and said, 'It is surprising to see the different rhythms. I gave her cold and summer, winter and swimsuit. I can see why she is so confused.'

'Fish,' she continued. 'A fish is quick, but sly and mute. I don't like fish, but I do like Judy. What is so *fishy* about her?'

Realizing the dual meaning of fishy, she began to laugh. Gabriela then commented on family drawing and on my observations as to the spatial organization of her colors and shapes for the family (i.e. who is close to whom, etc.)

'I know Judy's mother doesn't like me but I wasn't aware of it – she continuously calls me, telling me how dependent they are on my support... I can see the seduction going on between her and Judy and how enmeshed she is with her husband. Judy's mother, I don't really like and I can see why I have given her that terrible color. But I never thought how much destruction I see in this woman (shark, boots). The new husband, that is really interesting. I have never met him officially, maybe on one or two occasions when he brought Judy and Mum in. It is funny but yet I can see the potential of this man being a lion and also the dancing shoes, I can really see that this can be a good match for the "boots". As for myself, what can a snail do?...So slow, so fragile.'

I asked her: 'What about your other parts that are stone and party dress?'

Gabriela then looked at the chart horizontally. First we looked into the tempo we had there: wavy, slow, swift, gentle. She realized that her own tempo goes well with the mother, but not with Judy, although at times her tempo with Judy may appear to go well. More importantly, when it does go well, it is not because Gabriela is in tune, but because Judy waves according to Gabriela's rhythm.

The last thing we did with this chart was to look into the animal line: fish, shark, lion, snail. Gabriela was shocked to learn that Mum feeds on Judy. She was very curious to see that she can be with them in the same element, i.e. water, but how helpless she is in the struggle between the shark and the fish. She also noticed that in some cases snails could be the food for fish – although, she clarified, not her kind.

Gabriela was fascinated by the information her right hemisphere had given her about her encounters with Judy and Judy's family, but still she did not have a clear way to work with it. We then moved into the last part of our meeting where I asked her to tell me if she knew anything about the art of mixing colors. Gabriela shook her head. But when I reminded her of the basic 'rules' she exclaimed that she did know, for example, that blue and yellow together make green. I brought the color-mixing chart to help us out on this, and we were able to see what happens when the 'colors of the family' were mixed.

First we checked Judy and Mum: blue and dark brown. Combining the two, we got very dark brown, almost black. Gabriela said, yet again, Mum 'kills' her. Then we checked Judy and Gabriela colors together, blue and purple. The result was very bluish purple, a color that Gabriela liked. She said that it was a good gentle color that reminded her of pleasant times. When we examined Mum and Gabriela colors, it was obvious again that Gabriela 'did not have a chance'. The result was a very dark brown again, a color Gabriela felt was blocking her. It so happened that for the mixture with the mother's husband (B) both Gabriela and Judy got purple with a red hue. When Mum and B mixed, it was a very red brown. The result was, as Gabriela described it, a much livelier color.

Gabriela was at a loss. We started thinking about what could be the possible color for Gabriela to have when she meets with both Mum and Judy that will have any influence on them. After some thought, she said yellow.

We examined that, and realized that Judy will be green and Mum will be a lighter brown, maybe even ocher. I checked with Gabriela to see if that was a good solution, or better still, a good color for her to have. She smiled and pointed at her shirt, a very bright yellow, and said, 'For Judy, I should be a little lighter.'

We then examined what yellow meant for Gabriela. She said that yellow is energy, a clear head, sharp and to the point. I asked her where in her body could she feel that yellow. She pointed to the center of her belly. I then asked, 'Can you breathe with this yellow feeling, or show me how you sit with this yellow?'

She straightened herself up and said, 'I am breathing freely.'

I asked her, 'Do you know how yellow breathes, feels, thinks?'

She looked perplexed, so we explored the components of yellow for her to prepare the strategy of yellowness for her coming encounters with Judy and Mum. I asked her to visualize it and to feel it. I ended the session by saying, 'When you next see them, and you feel purple coming, go yellow instead.'

She smiled and said, 'Yeah, go yellow.'

This is an example of one of the techniques which I will describe here that make use of colors and shapes in order to 'interview' our right hemisphere. It is rather interesting how, for so long, we have neglected this wealth of knowledge, experience and absorption of impressions. We somehow were led to believe that only rational linear explanations are acceptable and correct. We have just seen, with the previous example, how much knowledge Gabriela had in store. She simply needed assistance to both trust it and to release it. I believe that most of it was already known to her – some was even on her mind – but the gentle approach and the fact that she came to the realization on her own made her so much more open to it. Another very important point to make here is that there was no interpretation or investigation of her unfinished business – her self-symbol as a snail, seeing the mother as blood. It could be explored, if she so wished, in a different session, and definitely with a different contract – for example, a therapeutic contract, not a supervisory one.

More color, shape, and line (C-S-L) techniques

Problem solved

Ask your supervisee to take three pieces of paper and some crayons. On the first paper, have him draw the problem or issues he feels are at the core of the case he brings to supervision in colors, shapes, or lines. Next ask him to draw the problem solved – how will it look? Last, ask him to draw what will happen in the middle.

Observe and discuss these three drawings carefully. Look for repeating colors and shapes and for changes in certain parts. Let the supervisee make dialog between picture 1 and 2, 1 and 3, 3 and 2 and see what comes up. Many times you will find innovative solutions in this process.

The way out (adapted from Mills and Crowley 1986)

Instruct your supervisee to:

Close your eyes and see an image of the problem you are struggling with. Put it somewhere at the end of a road, or on a hill, or on the edge of a map. Then imagine a figure or object that can solve the problem or make it possible to live with. Open your eyes. Take a piece of paper in any size you want, and draw the two images at two opposite ends. Draw an imaginative way or path between these two images. Divide the road into many parts, not less than 15, as in a children's game. Draw obstacles and pitfalls along that road. For each obstacle, make a card with a solution or task that can take the players across that problem so the game can progress. These can also be made as images or in writing. Give each of these solutions a number between 1 and 6. Take at least two buttons of a different shape or color for playing pieces, and a dice.

Invite your supervisor to play with you and see how you progress along the road to a solution. Whenever you hit a problem you'll need to get the right number on the dice corresponding to the number that appears on the solution card. I suggest that you take this opportunity to discuss the solution between you. If one of you gets the card the other will later need, you'll need to discuss that solution or an alternative one.

EXAMPLE: SUPERMAN AND THE MONSTER

Norma is a very experienced probation officer with broad training both as a counselor and as a family therapist. She has been coming to my supervision group for about five years. In the past year she has taken a very supportive role in the group, bringing new ideas from her systemic training to our meetings.

The case that she recently brought for supervision was a very sad story of a boy who was sexually abused by his father. Then, when taken out of the family (his father was imprisoned), he was placed in a 'home' for 'problematic children'. There, his uncle took care of him. Only later it was discovered that the uncle had also molested the boy sexually. The boy was very aggressive and non-cooperative. Norma was distressed. She said that she 'couldn't imagine herself crossing that mountain'. The boy had to be taken out of the 'home', but she did not really have an idea of where to take him or what to do with him.

I asked her to imagine the problem as an object or an image and visualize it somewhere beyond hills, mountains or cliffs. Then Norma imagined a figure who, in her mind, could make this a possible task to deal with. She then drew the two things. On one side of the paper was a dark monster in a cage; on the other side was Superman. Norma drew the road and the obstacles, some were 'real' like court and therapy; some were more imaginative that represented her fears. When she had to draw her 'solution cards' she found it challenging and asked the group to help her (Figure2.2).

It seemed as if this process alone was helpful for her and I felt no need to go on playing the game. But when Norma and some members of the group insisted on playing it and the rest of us observed, I must admit I was wrong. The actual playing was fascinating. Norma fought for solution cards that she had lost to her counterparts in the game; she smiled when she surmounted an obstacle. It was clear that the crossing of all those difficulties in the game made it possible for her to mitigate them in reality.

In our next meeting Norma reported that, despite the fact that she didn't use any of the solutions offered in her game, she was much more confident in the court meeting and actually secured for the boy a very good and therapeutic placement.

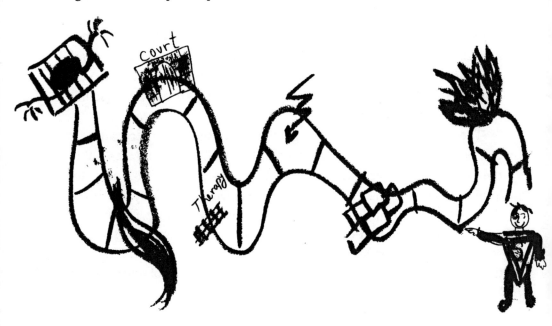

Figure 2.2 Superman's trail

We may feel disappointment that our 'magic' does not act in reality; but this is not the aim of any of these techniques. Nevertheless, if Norma got out of her 'loophole' and found the resources and strength to handle a very difficult case, I believe we have done our share.

CHAPTER 3

The Use of Stories, Films, and Plays in Supervision

I was asked to lead a supervisor's session for the Israeli Association of Group Therapy. It was a real challenge, I thought to myself: these people have hundreds of years of combined knowledge and experience, and tons of hours of supervision – what can I tell them? I went into my creative mode, and after some time came up with the following exercise which I have since used quite often. I call it 'looking for a co-therapist from the movies'. I will describe here the full version, although at times I use only parts of it.

Stage I

- Think about a difficult case in your therapy or supervision, someone you are concerned about or find difficult to handle.

- Now think about a character, a hero, or a small character (in a film, play, or book that you have seen or read) that you would like to have as a co-therapist.

- You may reflect on it for a few moments, or you may take the first person that comes to mind.

- If it is a film star then you may ask yourself in which film.

- It is better if you have both a female and a male character, but this is not essential.

- Turn to another partner (if it is a group supervision) and ask your 'hero' to introduce you to your partner. For example, what would Humphrey Bogart say about you if he were to introduce you?

- Then, introduce Humphrey Bogart and be sure to describe his characteristics.
- Describe the client you are concerned about and any important difficulties or encounters.

Now we have actually finished Stage I: the warm up, access to the characters and getting to know them.

Stage II

I ask the supervisee to imagine the following situation: You have asked the 'co-therapist' to join you for a session with your client. You set the time and date, but on that day you get a telephone call from the lottery company telling you that you have won the lucky draw of $5,000,000. You rush to collect your winnings and forget all about the meeting. Your co-therapist arrives at the meeting and meets with the client. Now, being you, later that evening, you remember where you were expected to be and you immediately call your client.

- She sounds_____, and says_____.
- What does he or she say about her encounter with your co-therapist? What are your client's impressions of that person. What did he or she get out of it?
- Anything strange he or she remembered from that meeting?
- Write all these things up!

Stage III

Next you sit and take a deep breath and the telephone rings. Your co-therapist is on the line telling you reactions and impressions of that session.

- What are the most important observations that your co-therapist made, and what are the things said or done that were meaningful (if any)?
- How did he or she perceive the client?
- What was the most unusual or embarrassing thing that happened in this session?

- In the role as your co-therapist, what are the main recommendations following that meeting with your client?
- List all these things!

Stage IV

Sit down and share these reactions and recommendations with your partner, or with the supervisor if it is an individual supervision. Which of the things that you wrote were confirming, new, surprising, or impossible?

Let us now look into a real supervision case I had recently.

EXAMPLE: A HOUSE FOR THE COCKROACHES

Dave is a very experienced psychotherapist with many credentials. He belongs to a group of expressive art therapists who meet once a month. This time he brought a case of a woman in her late twenties that he had been seeing for more than a year. She was a student with high expectations from her academic achievements. She was very disturbed – in his words, a borderline case. She would come every week, and had terrible fights with him. Sometimes she would humiliate him and attack him verbally, but at the same time he felt she was attracted to him. Moreover he was the 'only' friend she had.

When he tried to use metaphors or imagery with her she accused him of not really understanding her real-life situation. When he took her story literally, she said: 'Can't you see, these are not real cockroaches, but a metaphor of my problems.' The reality is that she lives as a student in a derelict house full of cockroaches and is 'looking' for a new house but 'unable' to find one.

Dave is a very experienced dramatherapist and Jungian analyst; he had used almost the entire repertoire of techniques and knowledge he has in order to achieve a breakthrough, but he was exhausted by her and felt stuck. When I suggested the 'movie co-therapist' he gladly accepted, though saying that he was rather skeptical.

Dave chose the psychotherapist from the film *Good Will Hunting* played by Robin Williams. He described the psychotherapist as warm and sensitive, but more than anything, down-to-earth, honest, and 'normal'. He said the psychotherapist employed unusual creativity. It does not matter if I perceive the character differently, it only matters that Dave saw him this way. When asked to explain what normal means, he said: 'Behaves like a normal person, behaves normally.'

I asked him to go through the different stages of not coming to the session and the telephone calls, as described in the technique above. After doing so, he said: 'She [the client] will be very upset that I didn't come. She will say that he [the co-therapist] is nice and understands her simply without all the games, the metaphors and all that. He knows what she needs.' Then he added: 'But she will say, "But he is shit, just like you."' When I asked him if she 'says' anything about meeting the co-therapist again, he said: 'No, she says, "I don't want you to bring him again."' Referring to the telephone call from his 'co-therapist' he said the following: 'She is a nice woman, she has a lot of problems. I think you should stop seeing her, put a limit to it.' Dave then smiled and said: 'I have long thought about it.'

I continued asking his reactions to other remarks, anything of the 'normal' recommendations. Dave said: 'You need to help her with her house; you need to do something practical with her.' He pondered for a moment and said: 'You know, I once tried to look for a house. I asked her to bring the newspaper and gave her the task of finding a house, but it didn't work.'

'Go on,' I said. 'What else would he tell you on the phone?'

A member of the group said, 'Maybe start with something simple. Maybe start with the extermination of the cockroaches. She needs to start with something small.'

Another member said, 'I think you should teach her how to build a "house" for the cockroaches.'

For the first time Dave smiled, even laughed. He said: 'The "house" could be a real one – the kind they use for cockroaches to be killed.' At the same time, he could use it metaphorically as an option for her to get friendly with them.

I then asked about the creative side of the co-therapist. Dave said: 'It is difficult for me to get into his role, but it is something creative in "normal" life.' I asked him if it could be a surprise, and Dave said yes. So I asked him what could be a surprise for her. He turned to the group for help. One member suggested that he should take her out for dinner. Dave laughed again and said that she would love it. Another member said: 'Perhaps you should give her a real reason to be angry. Maybe next time she comes, you let her knock at the door for a while and then open the door looking as if you have just woken up from a nap, exclaiming that you forgot all about your meeting.' Dave said that this was in line with the 'co-therapist' perception, something that can happen to a 'normal' person and that will be a realistic issue for her to confront. Another member suggested the 'surprise approach' and said maybe she called at the door just when you are taking a shower and you open the door with only a towel on.

One could be very critical about the way this supervision was going, but when I looked at Dave and saw the good laugh he was having, it indicated to me that 'fantastic reality' was in operation. He was relaxing; in fact his face looked much calmer, and he was able to relate to this difficult client with ease.

I then asked Dave to examine the different inputs from his co-therapist and consider how it feels now? Dave looked concerned and said that it helps just a little bit, because hers was a very difficult case. I asked him to recall all the suggestions that we made. He had forgotten that the first suggestions were to limit the therapy, to give her small tangible tasks, and to create the 'house for cockroaches'.

Dave indicated with his fingers that he felt a little better (the distance between his fingers was about 2 centimeters). 'Well,' I said, 'is that good enough?' Politely, Dave said yes, but it was obvious he didn't feel that way, so I asked him to envisage the scene that was most influential for him in the film *Good Will Hunting*. He immediately replied that it was the scene where the therapist held Will's throat and said: 'Don't you ever say that to me again.'

I asked him to position himself in this scene, to feel these same words, and to use the gestures and text to repeat it. Dave did this, once, but was not convincing either for himself or to the group. I asked him to locate in his body where he felt the sentence coming from. He said that it was in his stomach.

'What is its color or shape?' I asked him.

'Red!' he replied.

'Inhale red and think about that sentence; then position yourself and say it,' I said.

This time it was very impressive, and he said that sentence very convincingly. Dave smiled and said: 'OK, I understand something about this relationship, I must put boundaries and limits to it.'

I said to him, 'Before you go please remember the place in your body and the way your co-therapist sat and talked. Whenever you feel you are out of control, call Robin Williams in.'

At this point I asked Dave to check again to see how much help he got from the supervision. He showed with his fingers about 5 centimeters and said: 'For her this is almost too much. Yes, this is helpful.'

What really went on? Why was it different from another supervision? What could have been done differently? First, Dave is a very experienced therapist. I saw that he tried hard and that he had taken this case to supervision before. It was also quite clear that he would block straightforward 'countertransference' type supervision, and would not accept direct suggestions for action. The idea of asking him to imagine a fantasy co-therapist that he would have chosen to work with on this case was using several important components of the creative approach to supervision, and of the arts therapies in general.

1. **Distancing** We are talking through Robin Williams to Dave. Dave is talking to us, but more importantly to himself, through the fictional character. This technique frees the mind to examine the problem from a different angle. It enables us to say and explore things in a very playful way. Despite the fact that in our case I suspect that the real distance between Dave and the co-therapist was rather little, it was helpful for the group and for Dave. It enabled them to share countertransferential material without fear of criticism or judgment – for example, the bathroom scene.

2. **Taking on the role of the co-therapist** Experiencing the inner feelings and reactions 'in role' as the fictional character enabled Dave to get insight. He also got clues about how to 'stage' himself in future encounters with his client.

3. **The 'as if' reality, the ability to transcend into 'fantastic reality'** In fantastic reality everything is possible, all the limits and controls of reality are lessened, and one can explore ideas, actions, and emotions in a flexible way. This fantastic space allows and enables the group and the supervisor to explore options and alternatives, and to make suggestions without imposing them. In short, it is an invitation to play.

At times I will call upon a story instead of films as the agent for change. A story is a very good vehicle to bring new perspectives, new alternatives, and a fresh approach to a deadlock. A story has a very important component: it is there, remote, coming from far away. Many times we don't even know who wrote it (as in the case of fairy tales, legends, and myths). The story is always a quest, an attempt to find a way and sometimes a solution. And as much as these solutions can look simple and concrete, they also contain many symbols and metaphors. While listening to the story, one can get so many levels of understanding that can enrich the therapeutic encounter and even give strategic suggestions.

The most important part in my mind is the introduction of the supervisee to another supervisor – the 'big story', the old wise one that is an invisible yet tangible supervisor in the room. The 'big story' refers to the story that is beyond time, the story that repeats itself in a hundred different ways and, when identified, confirms so much. It opens up new options that linear thinking so often is blind to see and deaf to hear. Many times, the old wise part is so refreshing and new in the perception it offers, and in the simple way it perceives things, that it makes the complicated and the almost impossible into the simple and possible. Listening to the 'old wisdom' is a semi-dream-like experience; it takes the listener to the fantastic reality, and in a soft and soothing way it melts the resistance. The supervisee listens as an adult; and at the same time, his inner child listens too. We get the mutual effects of logic and non-logic processes.

EXAMPLE: THUMBELINA

Flora, a dramatherapist and social worker, was rather anxious when she came to our supervision group. A young woman, 25 years of age, was asking for her help. The client was dating a man who was a drug addict in remission. He had recently joined a rehabilitation community that, according to Flora, was more like a cult than a therapeutic institution.

Dina, the client, said she wants a stable relationship, that she was thinking of marriage, but her boyfriend wanted her to join the cult first. He said that they should live their communal life and see how it is; then, in the future, he might marry her. He pressured her to come along. Dina, wanting a man and family so much, was torn. She said that at her age she should be thinking about serious relationships leading to marriage and a family. She begged Flora to help her make the choice.

Dina was the younger of two girls. Until the age of 15, things were uneventful. At that time she started dating boys, most of whom had been involved in petty crimes and truancy and had smoked marijuana. Her last boyfriend before this one was an addict too. Her family didn't approve of these relationships and her father punished her. Further investigation indicated corporal punishments. She was not a bright student and went to a vocational school of clerical training, which she found boring.

Dina had another memory that Flora shared with us – Dina's father was close to her as a girl, training her to be a mechanic, which was his own profession. Flora said that she had noticed that Dina's physique was very masculine.

Flora posed a question: How should she assist this girl? She indicated that she doubts whether it would be short-term consultations, which was both Dina and Flora's superiors' expectation. Instead of jumping into questions and suggestions, I asked Flora to try to think of any story that this case brings to mind; she does not have to explain why she chose this story, and it doesn't have to directly correspond with the client's story. This was also the instruction to the group, though if Flora had a story, her story would overrule. Yet the group's stories would still serve us, as will be shown later.

Please note that the instructions are very important in so far as they are structured yet open-ended. There is no need to justify why this story or that character was chosen. Thus, it bypasses judgment and cognitive process, and allows the 'old wise one' to tell us stories.

Flora came up with the story of Thumbelina. On first reaction she said: 'I don't have a clue as to why I chose this story.' But I encourage her to trust the storyteller inside her. Still, I then asked the group to tell the stories they have as a reaction to Flora's account; they were Shakespeare's *As You Like It*, where the lady has to disguise herself as a man, and *Pippi Langstrum*, a Swedish tale about a tomboy. We then asked Flora to tell her story the way she remembers it.

Thumbelina is a very tiny little girl, so small she lives in a nutshell. She is very pretty and loved by many. One afternoon as she is taking a nap, a mother frog passes by her nutshell cradle. Seeing the beautiful little girl, the mother frog decides that she would be a wonderful match for her frog-son. She kidnaps the little girl and takes her to the river, where she places her on a huge lily. When Thumbelina wakes up she finds herself surrounded by water, and a huge ugly frog face staring at her. She is frightened when the frog-mother tells of her plans, adding that she is going to call her son to see Thumbelina.

When the frog goes away, Thumbelina starts to cry and a fish that is swimming by reassures her that he is going to help. He calls some fish friends to help in cutting the stem of the flower. The flower is set free and Thumbelina on it. The stream takes her quickly to the center of the river. She is upset again, when a ladybird comes and takes her on his back. For a moment she thinks it is a rescue. But no, he says he is bringing her to his family to marry her. Well she soon finds herself in a circle of bugs all humiliating her saying how ugly she is, and that they will not allow such a match. The bug takes her to the forest and leaves her there in the dark. Suddenly she sees a rat coming her way. This is a very old lady rat that said to Thumbelina: 'Come to my house. I'll feed you and you'll only have to clean my place.'

Old rat's house was underground, dark, huge, and dirty. Little Thumbelina had no other choice, so she works as hard as she can. In this dark house she meets a very sick swallow. Thumbelina takes care of him, feeds him and makes soft bedding for him, and finds a companion. When he grows stronger he flies away leaving Thumbelina all alone and miserable. For many days she works hard, crying and upset.

One day as she is crying, walking on the forest path looking for fresh leaves to put on rat's floor, she meets the swallow again. He sees her and immediately recognizes her. When she tells him how miserable she is he says: 'Climb on my back. I'll take you to a place where you'll be happy.' He takes Thumbelina to a land of light and warmth, and there on a beautiful flower she sees a little creature. A boy as small as a thumb and they fall in love and get married.

When Flora finished her story none of us in the group could believe how long it was, how she remembered all the details and more, so how could it happen that she brought such a story without preparation or planning. The first reaction was to the length of that story. My question was: 'Flora, do you still think it is a short-term therapy?' She didn't respond then, but later on she realized what I was asking.

I asked the group to tell what they hear in her story. The following is a short summary of the group's reactions.

First we notice the fact that it is a long quest, then that Thumbelina is actually the victim of circumstances. She is continually meeting the wrong groom, she is naive and can't protect herself. She has to work hard and learn to take care of someone else before she can really get help (perhaps an indication of a need to grow out of a narcissistic state). This is a story of abuse to a certain extent, a story where bad things are done in disguise of benevolent tendencies.

The other lesson is that quick solutions, the rescue or crisis intervention, are not really leading anywhere. Because as soon as the fish rescues her, the new trap comes along – the ladybird. So as much as this quick solution looks promising it is rather short lived. There were also some remarks about self-image, how she is so small and unfit, how she always gets 'involved with' or 'hooked on' the wrong groom. The story indicates that Thumbelina needs to learn to take care of herself before a real change can occur. And that marriage and family building is a reasonable target but not an immediate one.

Flora was overwhelmed by the amount of information 'revealed' in such a 'simple' story. We then looked into the way the 'big story' suggested we go about this encounter – understanding as well as goal-setting and strategy.

We immediately noted the pace. This time Flora could understand my earlier remark that it did not look like a crisis intervention. In fact it looks as if a short-term approach would soon bring Dina to the same place. So the pace should be slow and things should not be rushed.

There was a definite need to explore the patterns of Dina's engagements with men as the story indicated something that was reminiscent of Dina's previous encounters with them. Another concern and goal should be her self-image. She was getting support from the small size of Thumbelina and her inability to protect herself. But more than anything the story indicated that Thumbelina (Dina) needed to learn to care and invest in someone's well-being in order to grow. And that is certainly a worthwhile goal in therapy.

When we asked the rest of the group to say how the stories that the case had brought to mind could shed light on or add anything to the understanding of Dina's story, they came up with the following:

- *As You Like It* – The need to find one's own identity. The understanding that in order to survive one has sometimes to disguise oneself, but that it is only a temporary solution.

- *Pippi Langstrum* – The Swedish tomboy. Again a story about self-image and identity with a lot of rebelliousness and confrontation. Yet a willingness to belong and a need to make herself noticed.

It was rather interesting how these parts were all connected to Flora's story.

When the session was about to end I asked Flora to evaluate what she had gained. She said: 'A lot, so much reassurance of where I am and where Dina is. So much caution not to rush to quick solutions yet lots of respect for her wish to find a stable and long-lasting relationship. I don't know how I can 'sell' this idea of a prolonged process to her, but I'll surely try.'

Well, this was time for us to stop but we had some more minutes and I suggested the group think about a way to sell our understanding to Dina. After some joint efforts we came up with the following 'emphatic story that Flora should tell Dina'.

'I am very concerned about your story and request, and took it for consultation with a group of professionals including a professor of psychology and a psychiatrist. They all agree with your goal in life Dina. They think that it is right for you to want to build a mature relationship leading to the building of your own nest. They agree that going to live in this community that you're so afraid of, is not the best solution. When looking at your life story they see that you are right in saying that you are afraid to get the wrong partner, that your history does show that you tend to 'fall' into traps. Well, learning how to avoid traps is a process not a recommendation and we will need to learn to identify traps (even the ones that look tempting on first sight). And we will need to work on how you can become an active partner and not a passive recipient of things. But I would encourage you to choose a different path. A path that will not be short but will lead you to a better place where you will feel much more secure in the decisions that you are making.'

Flora was very satisfied with the process and the results of this session. She said: 'I got the answer I was looking for, I feel like saying "thank you and goodbye" now.'

This process, as much as it is impressive, needs to be taken very carefully. One must remember that we hadn't taken a full history of Dina nor did we have any psychological tests or other assessment of her psychological well-being. And we need to remember that Dina wasn't a patient, nor had she been referred by anyone but was seeking help for herself. Taking a distant perspective can be justified to get an understanding of a complicated case. But in no way is it a substitute for a thorough assessment.

The next examples will be of a short-term supervision with a group of professionals working under extreme conditions, and of a group supervision that was stuck.

EXAMPLE: ONE-SESSION SUPERVISION – HEIDI THE MOUNTAIN GIRL

I was invited to give a seminar in 1994 to some Bosnian therapists, psychologists, social workers, teachers, and physicians. They had come to Israel to learn about crisis intervention with children and the community in a situation of ongoing war. This seminar combined theory, skills, models, and supervision. One of the models that we discussed and that was later adopted extensively by the participants in their clinical work was the BASIC Ph model (Lahad 1992a), a model that will be described in detail in chapter 8. Suffice to use here a short explanation so that I can tell you about this unique opportunity to assist helpers in this terrible war.

BASIC Ph assumes that people cope with life in a variety of ways, but that with time everyone adopts their own particular preferred modes of coping. BASIC Ph is an acronym for the six underlying coping modes: beliefs, affect, social support, imagination, cognition (reality), and physical activity. For most people all these modes are present in greater or lesser degrees, but with some insight and testing it becomes apparent what a person's particular BASIC Ph makeup is. For example, one can be predominantly C, Ph, signifying the type of person who will wish to understand his or her problem then do something practical about it; or A, S, signifying the type of person who will wish to talk about his or her problem, and solve it preferably with others' help or within a defined social setting.

These predominant modes of coping constitute the language (in BASIC Ph terms) with which the person meets the world. In times of stress, it is important to adopt the client's personal language in order to create rapport and devise means of crisis intervention and practical support. Once other less strong modes of coping are identified, then further suggestions for treatment can be developed.

One of the Bosnian participants in the seminar, a pediatrician, described the case of a young girl rushed to hospital with epileptic symptoms after an air raid.

All tests were satisfactory, and after a few days she was about to be sent home; however, she was in a state of high anxiety. All the staff's attempts at calming her down were in vain. The girl had both parents and two brothers, one older and one younger. The parents were in favor of letting her stay in the hospital. After the parents had promised that they would move to another village, the girl left the hospital. The doctor was very worried that the girl might stay since there were many other children who really needed care. There were not enough beds and food for all of them, not to mention medicine.

A few days passed, and following another bombardment the girl was once more rushed to the hospital with the same epileptic symptoms. The parents left her in the hospital for the doctors to take care of. But once again, after extensive examination, they found nothing wrong. This time the girl refused to leave, the parents did not come to take her, and the staff members were at a loss as to what to do with her. With the girl still in hospital, the attempts of the supervision group to understand what was going on and to advise were met with the doctor's comment, 'We tried, but it didn't work.' My attempts at understanding the systems at work and the girl's outlook on the world did not advance progress.

The one new thing that we did understand was that the symptoms were in effect the girl's language of expression. Use of the multimodal BASIC Ph model gave us some guidance. We understood that the girl was using Ph, C, S (i.e. physical, cognitive, and social 'language'), but it seemed as if the doctor was finding difficulty in hearing the group's advice.

I turned to the group and asked if anyone could think of a story or legend in which something physical happens to a girl and she is sent away from home, and no one comes to take any interest in her fate. After a short silence one of the participants said 'Heidi'. I asked her to relate the story as she remembered it, I then asked, 'What do you think helped Heidi?'

She answered that Heidi helps another girl. I asked the doctor if that gave her any leads. She started to smile. 'It sounds right, we will give her something to do.' Other group members added that this would change her from being passive and dependent to being active and significant. The final suggestion was to promise the girl that she could come and take care of other children whenever she wanted to do so, but each time only for two or three days at most. In this way a number of things could be achieved:

1.   There would be no need for an epileptic attack: every time she wished to come to the hospital she was free to come.

2.   There would be no need for her to be passive and sick in order to receive attention.

3.   She would have a role and she could help. This constituted a change from an internal focusing on worries to an external one, worrying about the needs of others.

4.   Her regression would be structured to a period defined as active.

5.   She would acquire control over the symptom.

6.   Her situation would be reframed, from being a patient to being an assistant.

It was obvious that a second-degree solution had been found.

Reflections

One needs to understand the desperate situation in Sarajevo in order to appreciate the sort of work these helpers were doing. I believe that over and above what we call resistance (to authority) in supervision, the exhaustion of the staff and the daily encounter with disaster made it very difficult for the physician concerned to accept any advice from the group even though she herself asked for it.

BASIC Ph as a model for understanding human encounters with the world was very well received but did not open her up to listening to any new solutions or alternatives. The story as a neutral, indirect tool did not threaten her status or emotions. She found it amusing to listen to the story of Heidi and became receptive to Heidi's solution. Only then was she open to accept different interpretations of this, connecting it to her client's situation.

We countered the doctor's resistance by offering advice from the group by means of a story, seemingly distant and non-threatening.

EXAMPLE: THE LUCKY DRAW CLUB

I was supervising a group of sophisticated senior group facilitators, highly experienced people, and it was clear to me that avoidance would be the name of the game. The participants were reluctant to raise difficult issues and were very protective. One day no one brought up any subject and resistance was obvious. I then asked them if they could think of a story or film that could describe the supervision group. One of the group members said *The Lucky Draw Club*. I could feel people paying attention now. The

member then started to describe how the story, and even more so the film, was so much like them.

She said, 'You remember the old Chinese woman who said that Jews do not know how to play mah-jong?'

I asked her, 'Do you know how to play mah-jong?'

She smiled and said, 'I have this game at home and it is very difficult to play. It took me quite a while, it is from a different culture and philosophy.'

Other members of the group told what they remembered of the film *The Lucky Draw Club*, describing their opinions and impressions. They mentioned the need to continue playing the game – 'the show must go on'; the secrets that are so difficult to tell; the need to pretend and make-believe about the difficulties of settling in a new country; the question of translation (in the story the main character does not read and write Chinese and she needs assistance from one of her late mother's friends).

I then said to the woman who chose the film, 'So you think of us as the Lucky Draw Club.' There was great laughter.

Another member said, 'Yes, we don't know how to play mah-jong, do we'!'

I repeated, 'We don't know how to play mah-jong.' Another member said, 'We have difficulty in translation.'

Someone else added, 'It is difficult to open secrets here.'

We continued to talk about the similarities and differences between the story and us. From then on, we were known as the Lucky Draw Club. I must add that the name of the film in Hebrew can mean 'The Club of the Merry Luck'. It had changed the group into a much happier, much more active and vibrant group in which people opened up things and contributed willingly to the process.

The use of a known or written story

As early as 1987 Debora Kubobi wrote about the use of known stories in the process of supervising remedial teachers in the 'therapeutic teaching' technique that she developed (Kubobi 1987). Kubobi used known poems and stories, most of which describe adult–child relations, aiming at helping to sensitize young remedial teachers to the inner world and needs of the child as well as to their own psychodynamic processes. The structure of her supervision had three stages.

- Stage 1: Identification. After reading the story or poem the supervisee is asked to try to understand the inner world motivations and conflicts of the story's characters and their relations.

- Stage 2: Echoing. The supervisee is asked to look into two aspects: one is to find a character or issue that he finds close to himself – parallelism; and the other is to share how this is connected to any early or recent experiences he had.

- Stage 3: Disengagement. Gradually the supervisee is encouraged to reduce his emotional involvement, and he is encouraged to take a broader perspective and reflect on the applications of the story or poem in general terms in his daily work setting.

This is a very didactic approach, nevertheless I found it to be very useful with staff who need, to an extent, to keep their 'face saving' and façade in a rather competitive environment like school. Kubobi always had a story or poem ready to address issues that she thought needed to be addressed; but at the same time she was attentive to issues that were raised by the supervisees.

EXAMPLE: DRAKO THE LITTLE DRAGON

Karla is a special education supervisor and expressive arts therapist. One sunny day we were sitting outside in my garden discussing her workload and other matters concerning her workplace. Suddenly she said: 'I have this very difficult case. He is a boy in my therapeutic group of five very active boys. He is always against anything we do and talks like a martyr, saying to me and the group, 'This is my bad luck: in school nothing works for me, here you don't listen to me, the kids are calling me "pig", my parents are always scolding me, I am so miserable and I always do things that I don't want to.' Karla added that when he is given the chance he is very controlling and aggressive toward the rest of the group and immediately gets told off.

'What can you say about him?' She asked me. I had many ideas, but instead I told her this story.

'You see', I said 'a long time ago there was this little dragon named Drako who lived with his family of dragons. Drako grew up and he liked very much to spit fire. In the early days it was fun and OK, but as he grew up he was told off by his parents: not to blow fire any more at least at home or in public places. But Drako loved to spit fire, so every so often he used to forget himself and spit fire at home. And he was punished for that. Now when he reached school the teacher really didn't want fire and he was punished many times. But one day as he spat fire at school the class caught fire and his parents were called in only to be told that Drako would be expelled from school unless they put an end to fire-spitting.

'Drako had no choice and in no time he stopped spitting fire and then he forgot it altogether. He graduated from high school like the rest of the dragons and was looking for something to do in life. A job or something. He looked and looked but to no avail. Until one day he saw an ad in the paper saying that the king's treasury was looking for a new guard as the old one was about to retire. Drako thought this could be a good job with all the royal splendors that may accompany the job. So he applied and was accepted.

'The old guard was a very old dragon who welcomed Drako saying to him what a good job he had got. You only need to sleep here next to the safe and locks but I can tell you in my 55 years of service no one ever tried to burgle it. So the old dragon and Drako guarded the treasure for one night together and after that night the old dragon said he would now sleep in his bed next door and Drako would guard the safe.

'Well Drako was kind of glad to start and so he agreed and went to sleep by the safe. Suddenly in the middle of the night terrible frightening noises woke him. It was the sound of burglars cutting the chains of the first lock. Drako was so frightened he couldn't move. He saw the burglars working on the second lock. He froze. But when he saw that they managed to break this one and were now working on the safe's lock he tried to shout, but nothing. He tried again, but only a tinny ah sound came out. And the thieves were working without any fear.

'Suddenly Drako felt a tinkling feeling in his belly, and he tried again and a little flame came out, then he took a lot of air and a huge fire came rushing out of his mouth. The burglars were so frightened that they surrendered to him.

'The next morning the king and all the palace praised him, and his picture was in all the papers and magazines saying "Drako the fire-spitting dragon saves the king's treasure". I don't need to tell you what happened when his parents saw the article...'

Karla laughed and said, 'No need to.'

CHAPTER 4

Letter-writing and Imagined Dialogs

I didn't say goodbye

Gerald came to supervision after a long time in which we had not seen each other. By now he had a very successful clinic where he was doing mostly art therapy with young children. Already on the phone I could hear that he was not well. He told me that he tried to seek help from other colleagues in the clinic during peer supervision but nothing really worked. He had nightmares or bad dreams about a child that was in therapy and who died of leukemia before Gerald could say goodbye. He added, 'I probably need some grief therapy.'

Gerald is not usually the emotional type, he has a lot of creativity, he is very sensitive and good-humored but reluctantly shares feeling. And one very important thing is that children simply love this man.

I set a time for Gerald and we met in my room drinking tea like in the 'good old days' and eating some sugared nuts that my wife makes and Gerald always loved.

I then asked him to tell me about this boy that he came to talk about. Gerald looked as if he woke up from a dream and said: 'Yes, actually I came to talk about Eli.'

'Eli was a young boy aged eight who came to see me about a year and a half ago for behavioral problems. His parents were in the process of divorce when he was referred to me. He was diagnosed by a psychologist as a hyperactive child reacting to the impeding trauma of his family. A bright little boy with no learning difficulties. An only child to a very successful lawyer father and business manager mother. The interesting thing was that his teacher wrote that his behavioral problems were apparent as early as entering school. But no one took notice of it. So I was seeing Eli for about seven months, enjoying most of our meetings. He really was doing fine, he talked about his parents' divorce openly and we played a lot and painted a lot. His clay work was very indicative of his emotional state and he was rather aggressive with it. One day he made a body full of ants. I didn't know what he meant but he said it was those things inside that bother him. It was not long afterwards that his cancer was diagnosed and I was rather shocked that he might "know" of it before.

'His treatment was routine. Eli had chemotherapy and other medication and continued therapy. The sessions focused on treatment, coping, and cancer. Eli drew very big pictures in which he depicted his illness and the way to fight it. Though the doctors were concerned, he showed a significant improvement and stopped most of the treatment. Then about two weeks ago he had high temperature, was admitted to hospital and four days later died.'

Gerald was in tears. I asked him to continue talking but he said: 'I've said it all, I didn't say goodbye to him, I was probably the closest person he had in recent years. I didn't get to hospital in time. I thought I had time and I'd do it the next week. How can I talk to his parents? Of course they don't blame me, they don't even know how miserable I am. I know I am overreacting. I have that kind of help from my colleagues and saw how my early childhood is connected here. And I still don't find it any easier.'

My hunches were very similar to everyone else's who knew Gerald, and to Gerald's own introspection. I said to him: 'You came here for me to do something different with you and I was almost going to do with you more of the same. Let's do something that might be helpful.'

Following a short relaxation I asked him to imagine himself sitting in a serene landscape near a desk.

'Whether inside or outside, picture the situation and imagine that Eli is capable of hearing you now. Please talk to him in your head starting with the words "I just wanted you to know that I…". And when this is clear in your head take a piece of paper and write that letter. You may start writing with your eyes closed and only when you feel like it open them and continue to write for at least five minutes. If you find yourself stuck, write: "I still want to say things but it takes time for them to come so I am just waiting here until words come to me."'

I then sat quiet and left Gerald to write. Starting with his eyes closed he wrote for about eight or ten minutes, 'blindfolded'. I thought I saw tears pouring down his cheeks, because from time to time he took a tissue, but he immediately closed his eyes again and went on writing.

Gerald opened his eyes and continued to write for about five more minutes. First he was correcting his spelling and writing errors. Then he wrote some remarks and when he finished he looked at me and said: 'I am ready to talk.'

He read me the letter, which was a mixture of his own life story, and many things he wished to say to Eli. We talked about this letter for over an hour and then I asked him, 'What would you like to do now?'

Gerald looked at me for a moment and then said 'I want to hear his answer.'

Being so psychologically minded I said, 'Your father's answer?'

Gerald's look showed me how insensitive and patronizing I was. I smiled and said, 'You see how stupid I can be, go on and close your eyes, go back to where you met Eli in the beginning of the process. Look carefully around you. Try to notice everything around you, breathe normally and when ready, imagine or think about Eli. Then go into your inner ear and listen to whatever comes to mind. You may use the suggestions of the Little Prince. Look inside for the place where the Little Prince was seen last on this planet and then listen to the many bells of laughter coming from the heavens.'

Gerald smiled silently and I could see he was inside. After a while he opened his eyes and said, 'Yes, I can go home now.'

I asked him what he took from this process and he said, 'Permission'.

I looked at him. 'That is a lot,' he said, 'don't you think so?'

Free writing

Free writing is an excellent tool to be used in supervision, to enable expression of feelings, processing delicate issues and development of self-awareness. Writing is a way to communicate with oneself and with others. It is a natural and 'accepted' process, even for the more cognitive type of person. Cohen (1995) has written a whole book on the use of writing in self-therapy suggesting that 'free writing is our attempt to learn about our own masks and perhaps to try and look what is under them' (p.11).

In free writing the person is encouraged to write without planning or paying attention to grammar or spelling. It is a permitted way to get in touch with feeling thoughts and dreams. Free writing needs to be free of criticism, and thus enables expression of 'forbidden' or unaccepted thoughts, negative feelings and wishful thinking. I have found it very useful in times of extreme pressure to be a good preparation for coping with the unknown.

Bergman (Bergman and Witztum 1985) uses letter-writing as a form of free writing in family therapy helping his clients to part from unresolved relationships resulting from divorce or death.

This method can be a personal process of the supervisee to help him to face, reflect, and ponder on issues in his work. It can also be material to work on in supervision, either when done during supervision or sometimes as preparation for the supervision session.

A very important part of writing is the ability to go back to it on different occasions to look into what was written, react to it, debate it, change it or just reflect on the process.

More self-writing exercises

Letters that will never be sent

Ask the supervisee to write a letter to a client especially following a very difficult or loaded session. The instructions are as follows:

> This letter will never be sent nor will it be read by your client. Later on you will decide which parts, if at all, you wish to share with me. We can also discuss the process only and an image or a sentence that is of significance for you.

Once the supervisee has written her letter, ask her to read it again and underline all the sentences, words, or images that she liked in her letter. Then if she wishes, she can either read and discuss the whole letter or she can share any of the sentences, ideas, or words she finds meaningful in the letter. This can also be the basis of a role play between supervisee and 'client'. The supervisee will decide which part she will play, using a technique that we will describe later as a psychodrama tool – 'talking to an empty chair'.

At times the supervisor can suggest that the supervisee read her letter quietly and then close her eyes, listen to 'the reply' and write a letter from the client to her. This could be a very good way to get an insight into the client's needs and sometimes even to the strategy of how to go about addressing them.

A good way to end up the session could be to ask the supervisee to write down all the sentences and words she marked and see if any of them make sense for her now.

EXAMPLE: SEPARATION VS. ABANDONMENT

A colleague of mine asked me one day to run a supervision group for child protection officers. All of them were very experienced and had a huge workload. She said that some were showing signs of 'burnout' being irritable and short tempered. In my first session with this group I was exploring with them their professional self-image. The result was a bridgeable gap between their ideal perception and reality. So in the next session I asked them to draw on two sheets of paper, an image of 'separation' and an image of 'abandonment'. I then asked them to write their associations to these words and to share it with their peers. The last part of this exercise was to sit in front of any of the images they drew and imagine a child in their care that they either had to separate from or they felt that they abandoned. Sitting in front of that image I asked them to write to this child a letter 'that will never be sent'.

This had a very moving effect. Some of these 'stiff upper lipped' people opened up and shared moments of despair, moments of being alone – as one woman said: 'Just me and God.' Some shared with us their letters and wanted to hear our comments, and one asked the group to write her an answer as if they had been the boy to whom she had written her 'unsent letter'.

The inner dialog

The following examples are self-correspondence techniques, which in a structured way enable the writer to air his views openly. These may sometimes serve as an inner preparatory step aiming at clarifying relations between supervisor and supervisee as well as a method to discuss and enhance their relationship.

How do I see?

Please divide the paper into four parts. In each part please write:

1. That is how I see myself...

2. That is how I see you...

3. That is how I see you perceiving me...

4. That is how you see my perception of you...

You may use it only as a ventilation technique or as a starting point for discussion.

Sentence completion

1. If only you agreed...

2. I would like to give you...

3. I cannot give you...

4. I know you expect me to...

5. I know that sooner or later you will find that I...

6. I have to show that I...

7. I expect of you to...

8. It's hard for me to say to you that...

9. I am embarrassed when you...

10. My wish is that you...

11. My best defense against you is...

12. When I say goodbye I...

EXAMPLE: CLARIFYING EMOTIONS

Josh and Sara had been co-leading a group of wife batterers for the last five years. When they started coming for my supervision it seemed as if they were a very cognitive 'couple' and the strategy they were using with these men was also very cognitively oriented. It was obvious that despite this 'cognitive' appearance they had lots of unresolved issues that are very much part of co-leading a group. However, my attempts to check 'how did they feel about it' didn't lead very far. So I said to them I had this new questionnaire just out in the market that is very useful for co-therapists. I then gave them the above sentence completion list.

Josh took it very seriously and asked if he could work on it at home; whereas Sara said she'd rather do it now and see what happens. Josh reluctantly agreed. I said that there was no time limit, but that I assumed it would take about five to ten minutes to complete.

Josh found sentence 5 'I know that sooner or later you will find that I...' a very difficult sentence and skipped it. Sara laughed and said she completed it. '...that I am a very intolerant person when it comes to violence.' When I looked somewhat puzzled she added, 'Yes, they expect us to be tolerant, but when I hear these men I myself become very aggressive, so how can I be a therapist when I can't tolerate these men's behavior?'

Josh said to her he never thought that it was intolerance he just felt that she had more confidence in running the group and that is why she is more active. It was quite obvious that Josh was afraid to look at the feelings this group provoked in him, and maybe even feared losing Sara as a partner; and as we continued looking at the 'questionnaire' it became also clearer to him. He chose to share sentence 6: 'I have to show that I am strong and able to help these men change their behavior. If they will perceive me as weak I am lost.'

As we read the sentences together the cognitive process of sentence completion turned into a value and emotion clarification process that opened up a long journey of joint work for Sara, Josh, and myself.

Me and myself

At times it is difficult for the supervisee as much as it is for the supervisor to open up things between them. The following exercise is very helpful to many. This can also be done on your own to make you more aware of the masks you put on.

Take two pieces of papers and write on top of one: WHAT PEOPLE THINK OF ME? Then write down anything that comes to mind. Take the other paper and write: I AM REALLY... Then write down everything that comes to mind. Another version of it could be: MY IDEAL THERAPIST IS..., BUT I AM REALLY...

When you have finished writing the lists, sit down, alone or with a counterpart. Put the two papers one next to the other, and either make a dialog between the two or let your partner ask any question she feels needs clarifying and let the different part answer. If you write down this dialog, you may be able to look through the whole process and evaluate it once you have finished. And if you do it every so often throughout the supervision sessions, you can trace changes as well as repetitive issues and use them as part of the supervision process.

Where would I like to be in six months' time?

This is an exercise that can be done with a supervisee both as a contract procedure between the two of you, or to help him clarify goals for his work with a client, group, or family.

Read the above question. Try to cover every possible area, don't judge if your wishes are possible or not. Once you set your imagination free and take risks you will be surprised how much is possible. So think about the case you are concerned about and write all those things that you wish to happen in six months' time. Think about yourself in these relations, about yourself as a therapist…anything you wish to concentrate on is fine.

You may mark your list in two different ways:

1.   By order of priority, maybe by giving each one a number

2.   Possible, maybe possible, I've gone nuts…

Sit with your supervisor and explore the lists.

The magic wand

This technique is very well known as the solution-oriented therapy (de Shazer 1985) but can easily be used as a self-writing technique.

- Think about a client of yours about whom you are concerned.
- Close your eyes and imagine that during the night an angel from heaven came down to that client and kissed him on his forehead.
- Next day, without him noticing, the problem has gone.
- What will be the first and smallest thing that you will notice that has changed overnight?

- Have you ever noticed that thing in your client? When? Do you know what caused it then? Can you repeat it or help it to reappear?

- You now have the first step on the ladder of change. Work toward the smallest visible target of change with your client to bring about change.

- When you discuss it with your supervisor try to understand the underlying mechanism beneath the desired behavior.

EXAMPLE: TED

It was one of those days when third-year dramatherapy course students are exhausted and at the same time finding it difficult to believe that in a few months' time they are out there in the world of psychotherapy on their own.

Pat was in this very mood as a result of a very difficult case of a hyperactive child's mother accusing her that 'nothing happens'. So I asked Pat to close her eyes and imagine that day that Ted will come and she will see a small yet significant change in him, as if an angel came down from heaven and kissed his forehead and suddenly it happened.

Pat smiled and said, 'Yes, he will be able to stay in role.' I said to her to pick some smaller and clearer behavior.

Pat closed her eyes and said, 'He will come to my room, sit next to my table, and we will be able to plan our session.'

'Good,' I said. 'Did it ever happen, did you ever experience that behavior from Ted?'

'Yes, once a long time ago,' Pat said. 'Since then he is always coming in like a storm.'

'What was the thing or things that happened then, can you recall?'

Pat thought for a while and said that she was more relaxed then, and it was the time when she had more contact with Ted's father. 'Oh well,' she added. 'His father is even more frustrated.'

We analyzed the different possibilities and ended the supervision with two options: 1) A guided fantasy for Pat to see herself in the situation where Ted is more responsive; 2) A telephone conversation with Ted's father talking about him taking a more active role again. With these two activities we left Pat to continue her work with Ted.

A quick note

This exercise is rather useful when you want to help yourself or your supervisee to see what is the most important thing they would like to say or what is the most important goal he would like to set for that client or group.

You somehow have to leave without any warning, so you quickly scribble a note saying:

'Sorry I had to rush, I don't have much time to write. I only wanted you to know…'

CHAPTER 5

Images and Guided Fantasy

Metaphors

Supervision can be at times a very tiring business, even for the most creative person. So when this happens to me I opt for another angle of the metaphoric work. I ask my supervisee to think about his client or clients, which may be a family or a group, as a mechanism such as a machine or a car, or as a system or organization such as a factory or a circus. It can also be a place such as a central bus station or an airport. When my supervisee chooses the metaphor we explore it, using many questions as will be demonstrated in the following example.

EXAMPLE: A CAR IN A FUNFAIR

Liz was a senior social worker, supervisor and deputy director of a drug rehabilitation center. She worked there for the last ten years. She joined my supervision group for supervisors because she felt she wanted to share her experiences and concerns with a group of highly qualified people. We used to meet every fortnight for a three-hour consultation. Each time a different person brought a case for discussion. As happens with very qualified and experienced staff they tend not to prepare the case in advance, preferring to rely on their intuition, experience and virtuoso abilities. I must admit that despite my continual efforts to make them commit themselves in advance to bringing a case I failed, but nevertheless enjoyed that group a lot.

It was yet again Wednesday afternoon, a rainy day, and of course no one had prepared a case for the group. (Some might interpret it as resistance, others as a challenge to my creativity and improvisation abilities – I opted for the latter.) Liz volunteered to bring up a problem. She was working with a very difficult group of workers. She was their superior, responsible for guiding the staff consultation and supervision meetings, and found the staff very difficult to handle.

I gave her the above suggestions and she said, 'They are like a car. No, they are lots of passengers in a car.'

I asked her, 'Please describe that car.'

'It is a beetle,' she said. 'An old cracky beetle car.'

'Do you see anybody at the wheel?' I asked.

'Yes,' she said. 'But it is almost impossible to run this car as it is so crammed up. They are all hovering around the poor driver, the car is full of people.'

'And how does it look from the outside?' I asked.

'As if it is going nowhere, there is a feeling that the car is going in circles.'

'And where are you?'

'I am watching from the outside. Hold on a minute,' she said. 'It is not a regular car, it is a car in a funfair.'

She continued to describe it, 'There are few cars, they are going like in circles banging into each other.'

'And where are you?'

She smiled and said, 'I am the controller.'

So I said, 'Can you control the pace of this race?'

'Yes,' she said. 'I can decide whether there is electricity or not.'

I asked her to look at the ring of little cars and try to see how they are organized. 'Are they all on one side? Are some drivers more careless while others are avoiding clashes? Can you see if any of the drivers are closer to the control point than others? Is there anyone challenging the controller's authority?'

Liz continued to close her eyes and looked very serious. She looked and looked and we waited for her to share what was going on. When she opened her eyes she looked quite bewildered. A friend made a remark to that effect and Liz said, 'Yes, I know what became clear. More than anything I saw the ones who were calling the controller to shut off the electricity and the one who objects to it. This is very interesting because I thought he was very instrumental for that group. Of course I sometimes felt or suspected that he also has a negative influence, but in the image it was clear that he is sabotaging things.'

We went on exploring the different parts of this image and then I asked Liz if she was willing to explore other aspects of the situation and she gladly agreed. So I asked her to close her eyes again to look at the mini-car ring, to see it all working and the controller in his booth. I then asked her to accelerate the speed so that it would all go very quickly and to see what happens. Then I asked her to slow it down to 'slow motion'. And then to put it back to normal and turn the controller around, looking away from the ring. The last part was very difficult so I asked her to open her eyes and sit with her back to us while we enacted the scene. This of course was a dramatization of her part. Liz was surprised that after a few minutes she could let it happen.

The feedback she gave us when we finished dramatizing was that she felt awful, mainly for the sake of those who needed her support. And when she heard the group noise and couldn't turn to see, she really felt frustrated. But then came some relief as no real disaster happened. The group told her that they were looking for her guidance to a certain extent (apart from the 'troublemaker') but when she didn't come back, they learned to cope. They avoided clashes and even enjoyed the tension.

When she heard how the group coped with her 'absence' she said, 'I suppose there is something for me to change too.' Liz evaluated the process saying that at times it was a dream that turned into a nightmare, but the fact that she had it 'under control' certainly clarified things for her. She specifically mentioned her confirmed awareness as to the role of the 'troublemaker', her own need to control and her new experience of 'letting go'.

The next case is taken from group supervision for dramatherapists. This time it was a rehabilitation program for chronic patients following discharge from a psychiatric unit.

EXAMPLE: LIFEGUARD IN A COFFEE SHOP

Sara was a dramatherapist who had been working with a particular group for two years. The previous year her group had been such a success that they asked her to continue it for another year. The members had not changed much, but somehow Sara felt it was not going so well. The week before the supervision it was even worse. She said, 'Two of the patients fell asleep in the middle of the session. And I know it was not because of their medications.'

Sara also told us how upset and disappointed she was that the group is so dull this year. I asked Sara to describe the group as a place or a happening, and she said, 'It is a coffee shop.'

'Where is that coffee shop?' I asked.

'On the beach,' she said.

'Where are the people? On the beach or in the coffee shop?'

'Well, very few are in the coffee shop maybe two or three, the rest are on the beach.'

'Are they in the water, on the seashore, lying down, playing, eating?'

'No, they are all on the beach, perhaps one or two are putting their toes in the water but most of them are hanging around the lifeguard's shed. In fact the lifeguard and his assistants are next to them. It is too dangerous to leave them like that by the sea.'

'Did anything happen for them to need such guarding?'

'No, not yet.'

'Does the guard have experience in such matters?'

'Theoretically yes.'

'What do you mean?'

'Well he is rather new and has never before had to perform a sea rescue, maybe in his days in lifeguard training school.'

'So it is a very difficult job.'

'Oh, it is a hell of a job.'

'What about the ones at the coffee shop.'

'They don't really mind. They don't want to go to the sea. They are sitting half asleep in the coffee shop.'

One of the group members asked Sara, 'And who are you in this story?'

'The lifeguard of course, isn't it clear?'

'And your co-therapist?'

'The coffee shop owner,' she said. Then she burst into tears.

Sara said to us, 'Last year I was the shop owner and my co-therapist was the lifeguard. This year I was made the lifeguard but I know nothing of lifeguarding. My coffee shop was so successful we had such a good and meaningful time.'

'Why did you accept the new role?' someone asked.

'No one really asked me. I assumed that as I became a full member of staff I should be on guard.'

I asked her to tell us about her role at the coffee shop.

'Well, it was creative and fun. We did so many new things; they all loved it and never missed a session. They were so lively we couldn't believe it. Even the ones who never shared a story before, not to mention taking part in a play or acting, were slowly becoming part of that group. I must go back and talk to my co-therapist and discuss it with her. I can't and don't want to be a lifeguard. I am very good at the coffee shop and in fact she is a good guard.'

Sara was still in tears but it looked as if she knew where this session was going to take her.

A few weeks later when she came to our group she said, 'The coffee shop is back in business.' She added, 'I managed to discuss it with my co-therapist, she was really helpful yet we agree that sometimes she will also mind the shop and that I'll try and learn some lifeguarding techniques. But we are back in our special coffee shop.'

We learned that there are difficult times in the 'coffee shop' but that Sara, her co-therapist, and the group are coping with them in a mature way.

Sometimes we fulfill expectations that were never meant for us nor were we ever asked to perform them. At times we are pushed to do things we are not good at or don't like doing. It was fascinating to see how this process led Sara to so much insight and understanding. Without any imposition or judgment or criticism. As Sara chose the metaphor, and just like Liz before, she was committed to it and was willing to explore its many facets.

It is amazing to see that when a supervisee or a client chooses the image or metaphor, they are much more open and willing to take risks and explore its many facets. An individual example of that same process was when I asked one of my supervisees: 'What is the image you have when you think about that client? Can you think of any animal or creature?'

He said, without any hesitation, 'A snake.'

'Where do you see it?'

'Out in the field crawling and making this terrible "sssss" noise.'

'And where are you?'

'Oh, I am high above. I am a butterfly.'

'So he can't hurt you.'

'Yes, but I am short lived...'

And so we went on in this procedure using the fantastic reality as our stage before re-entering reality and 'making sense' of it.

Sculpting, role play, and enactment

A useful and revealing experience for many supervisees is the use of various dramatic techniques. By giving the situation an almost 'real life' size, doing it with their own bodies, enacting their own part or someone else's part, it gives a combination of both physical and emotional experience.

- **Sculpting** – a technique that uses the participant's body and any other object in the room together with gestures, sounds, and movements to represent an inner or real issue, (e.g. mood, feeling, reaction, metaphor) in a sculpture-like form.

- **Role play** – a process of giving the participant a chance to play someone else's role, to 'get into his shoes' and get both cognitive and affective perceptions of the character played. Role play allows the participant to evaluate his previous encounter with a specific client as much as to prepare for a future encounter in a form of 'rehearsal' for that imagined meeting. Many times it is used to solve or process 'unfinished business' with a living or dead person.

The next exercise is very useful either with an individual supervisee or with a group, when facing a barrier, obstacle, or 'resistance', both from within and without. It is a combination of guided fantasy, free writing and sometimes dramatherapeutic enactment.

The wall

In a soft voice I say to my supervisee:

> Find a comfortable space, sit or lie down. Feel the pressure of your seat or floor against your body. Listen to your breathing… In a few minutes we are going to set out on an imaginary journey. Listen to my voice and try to visualize the story. If you lose the thread of the story – don't worry. When you hear my voice again you can continue your journey. It is a nice day, the weather is mild and the sun is shining. We are off on a short trip. The road winds through vast pastures and green shrubs. The sky is bright, and a few soft white clouds float up high. The trail is clear and easy to follow… We are approaching a grove, almost as thick as a wood. As we enter the shade of the trees we feel a refreshing coolness. The sunshine through the foliage, imprinting light patterns on the ground. As we start our walk into the grove, the road splits into several paths. Each of us chooses his or her own path. The paths weave among the trees. At times the thicket is so dense that odd branches scratch you. At times the road is clear. At times it becomes dark and moist. At times it is really bright. Follow your own path. Then suddenly there is A WALL! You wonder what this is, blocking the road. The path stops at the foot of the wall. The wall is surrounded on both its sides by wild and thick growth. You stand facing the wall,

looking left and right for a way around it – but there isn't any! You notice birds flying over the wall, coming and going.

Now, sit facing the wall, close your eyes and talk to it. Tell it how you feel being here, in front of a closed, sealed wall.

After this I say to the supervisee:

Open your eyes. You will find different materials such as Plasticine, cardboard, paints, papers, Lego blocks, and other odds and ends. Start working: build or paint a wall, using the different materials. Pay attention to details: the stones, the height, the surroundings… Pick up a piece of paper, write down whatever you feel and experience right now.

The next stage is sharing the image and writing with one's group and then asking them to sculpt for you the 'wall' you met. The supervisee may help them to 'build' that wall by adding his dimensions or asking the group to use objects such as chairs and tables. He then sits in front of the wall, reads his passage and has three chances to cross that wall.

Figure 5.1 The wall

At the end of these three trails each one sits down and writes any image, words, or sentence that was meaningful for him in the enactment. Finally, each member can share these reflections and the group may talk about the meaning of this exercise in their life.

One of the very important parts of supervision is to help the supervisee assess the group's situation at a given time. A very useful tool for group assessment is sculpture or dynamic representation of the process through enactment.

The following exercises, all adapted from Jennings (1986), are very much a combination of dramatherapy and sociodrama. They can be done with the supervisee during supervision, or as an evaluation given by the supervisee to the therapy group for later discussion in supervision. As with many of the techniques in this book, they can also serve as self-evaluation methods.

The swimming pool

The instructions are:

> Imagine that your group is at a swimming pool. Some are just arriving, some are in the cloakroom or changing room, some are in the water, some are outside the water, some have an official role such as pool attendant, coffee shop attendant, lifeguard, etc.
>
> Draw a general layout of the premises and mark on it where you see each member of the group and yourself.

If this exercise is done with the group then the following options are available:

1. Each member draws his own map, and later on they discuss it using sculpting and enactment to assess the meaning of each map.

2. A huge map is drawn and each member places herself on it.

3. The room is the swimming pool and each member places himself in this space.

EXAMPLE: THE UNGUARDED SWIMMING POOL

David was a social worker in a drug rehabilitation centre. He used this exercise with a supervision group. To start with he drew a map of the group positioning some in the shallow water, some on the chairs outside, one or two in deep water, one as the wardrobe attendant, and two on the diving board. Then he asked the supervision group to sculpt it for him. It was only at this stage that David realized that there wasn't any lifeguard in this pool. He actually forgot to put one in. He smiled and said to the group 'the lifeguard wishes to be off-duty', putting himself as the lifeguard on a deck chair. Examining the situation from that position he said: 'No, too early to leave that pool without a lifeguard but it is definitely something I wish I could afford sometimes.' We then went into examining different options of being a lifeguard in this swimming pool.

The bus

The same method can be done either as a bus or a train. The instructions are:

> Imagine that your group is a bus. Please place yourself anywhere in this bus. Driver, passenger (where in the bus do you sit?), still waiting at the bus stop, inspector, etc.

This exercise is best used when each one chooses their role and then they improvise what is happening in that bus. Many a time this becomes a very dynamic processing of the group's self-perception and also an important catalyst for change.

Family secrets

At times you may find that by helping your supervisees to improvise or role play a situation things will be clearer. Role play allows them to see their client's point of view and the many facets of the situation, clarifying issues like motivation, hidden agenda, coalitions, and oppositions.

In 'Family secrets' the supervisor invites the supervisee, who brings a case of a family to the supervision group, to ask members of the group to 'create' the family, and to decide what secret that family chooses to keep hidden.

Characters: A family (members to be decided).
Scene: Family living room.
Action: The family have an unhappy or guilty secret (they may know what it is from the supervisee or improvise on their own). This may take up to eight minutes.
Let them play the situation and the supervisee to direct them when needed. At the end let each participant share what it was like to be in this situation and what insights they had as a result of the experience. Then let the supervisee reflect on the process. If needed, let the group replay part of that scene or all of it.

Polarities

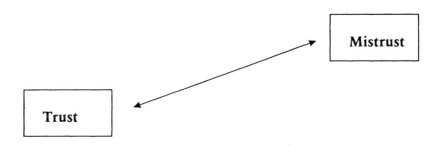

Figure 5.2 Polarities

The following exercise can help the supervisee to clarify the situation in the therapy group she leads.

The supervisor invites the supervisee to place others on a diagonal between polarities (for example of trust) as he perceives his clients, each of the participants representing one member of her therapy group. If however she is short of people she may use objects too (Figure 5.2). Individuals should then be allowed to respond to where they have been placed.

Then the supervisee is asked to place herself on this continuum and to make the following statement: 'Other people see me as…whereas inside I always feel…'

Chair sculptures – Important people

The supervisor explains that chairs are to be used to represent people who are, or have been, important influences in the lives of members of the client's family. A maximum of four chairs should be used. The supervisee should identify positive as well as negative influences.

In turn, supervisees should sit in each chair they have assigned a role or position to and 'introduce them' by doubling. That is to say, they should speak on behalf of the person represented, saying how that person has influenced the client, for whom supervision is sought. When all the chairs have 'spoken', the supervisee should respond by saying something to each of those 'important people'.

At the end the supervisee shares with the group what messages or ideas he can take back to the therapy session with his client.

CHAPTER 6

Sailing into the World of Magic –
The Use of Therapeutic Cards

Therapeutic cards are not necessarily the prepared cards that I mention in this section. Although I have found the variety of cards and activities that can be played with them fascinating, one can easily make one's own set of pictures or images and still have the same projective and introspective result.

It is important to say that historically there have been many projective techniques such as Rorschach inkblots, TAT (Thematic Apperception Test), CAT (Children Apperception Test) and HAT (Human Apperception Test). All the cards represent different situations where adults and children are encouraged to tell stories for diagnostic purposes. Violet Oaklander (1970) uses TAT and CAT as probing and storytelling cards rather than diagnostic tools.

The cards that I work with have been developed by a psychologist and an artist, taking into consideration various options and elements that are important in the therapeutic encounter. One can easily make one's own set of cards from postcards, journals, etc. However, there is a benefit to the use of 'commercial' cards, in that these cards look official and 'neutral', thus are respected as all printed material to be objective, reliable, and valid. With some clients it has a significant effect, others may suspect it is some kind of test.

SAGA – Therapeutic storytelling cards
(adapted from Ayalon (1997))

SAGA cards depict characters, scenes, and objects from a land and time that never was and always is. Each card is a springboard for a story. They are intended to awaken the delight of surprise and to rekindle memories of childhood dreams. SAGA cards offer the opportunity to exercise the imagination, have fun, even play – without needing to win or score points. With this in mind the storyteller in all of us is encouraged to take a SAGA card and begin to spin a yarn…

> Can you remember sitting next to a loving adult listening to a story told especially for you? Sometimes the tale made no sense at all: it just made you laugh or shiver, sometimes it encouraged you to make up your own ending or change the beginning. Sometimes it made you wonder. We all remember the tried-and-true fairy tales, the ones we never doubted and never will doubt. Those stories left us breathless and ready for more, and filled our memory with a range of special images: Rumpelstiltskin, Snow White and the Seven Dwarfs, Hansel and Gretel… These stories are generation connectors, grandpas and uncles know them and they can be told over and over again. Their retelling rolls off our tongues without effort, and our hearts are still warmed by them.
>
> The SAGA cards directly and indirectly refer to classical fairy stories and heroic tales and myths. Each card suggests some scene in some story or tale. So, whether a SAGA card prompts us to retell the story of Sir Lancelot or one about the maiden and Babayaga, or whether it leads us along a new path in search of the Holy Grail, we have entered the special world of universal myths. These are the stories that, if we choose, provide us with the opportunity to venture into the interior landscape of our self. The universal myths can never be untold. They are there for us, with all their insightful beauty…just down the road and around the corner…in the land of fantasy.

Let me start by sharing with you one option of warming up your supervisees to the fun of playing without competing.

Allow your creativity to flow and skip about in time, space, context and meaning. Tell the story in an active tense, keep the events moving along. Be yourself, and the temptation to impress people with your wit and literary skills will vanish. Especially in group play, you may want to agree upon certain courtesies, such as time limits, not reinterpreting another's card, or interrupting each other. In some circumstances it may also be a good idea for a player to have the choice of *not* playing a card, to pass without comment or padding.

In pairs or small groups each player, in turn, draws three (or five) cards at random and inspects them. If a card is not liked, it can be put upside down next to the player and another card taken at random. Now the three (or five) cards are set down in a row – not necessarily in the order drawn. The player then develops a story based on the cards, the beginning suggested by the first card, and the ending by the third (or fifth). When the story is completed other players may ask questions to clarify their understanding of the story. The 'teller' is encouraged to reflect on the process and see if the way the story deals with the issues raised in the 'saga' corresponds to known ways of meeting challenges or problems. At the end the player may return to any rejected card and ask what was in it that made her reject it? Was that issue addressed later on by her story anyway?

Your personal Saga

The procedure described here is an example for a longer process where the supervisee uses his imagination first as a playful element, second as an exercise for the right hemisphere and third as an opportunity to be introspective about what is going on in the therapy, or supervision, or both.

Each day, over a specified period (month, six weeks, etc.), set time aside to write a segment of a story in a journal or bound notebook. Draw a SAGA card at random and write at least a page-long segment of the story, starting the first day with 'Once upon a time…'. During the writing reread only the previous day's entry. Do not attempt to generate a coherent, well-plotted story. Let the mood of the day dictate the direction of the story and remember that you are in a magic world where everything is possible. Drape yourself in the mantle of witch, monarch, or *deus ex machina*.

Indulge in lapses of memory, relish your obsession with details you would otherwise deem unimportant, rename characters, change their roles, status, color, gender, or species. Kill the hero and resuscitate him in a new role. When the specified period of time is over, end the story.

Set aside an evening and read the whole thing through. Resist the temptation to annotate, edit, correct, censor. Decide whether you want to read the story – or portions of it – to your supervisor or to your group. In any event look at it from the point of view of an observer who looks in on the story as if it were an account of where you were during this period of time with the different clients or encounters. Let that observing part of you mark all the images, sentences, words, etc. that it finds attractive in the story and use them as guides to the process. If you wish you can share this part or parts.

Defining the problem and finding solutions

Sometimes we need a special technique in order to get out of a mess, or when we feel there is a need for a process that is helpful with supervisees who are either very reserved or who talk too much. In the former case it helps you to interview and in the latter it helps you to focus. One must remember, however, that the process that is described here needs to be used carefully, especially when the supervisee is a spiritual type or already tends to perceive the supervisor as a 'mindreader.' It is a powerful tool but needs a delicate approach.

Now because we are in the 'fantastic' world of cards and want to make use of its unexpected, surprise element, we are structuring the procedure to ensure that our supervisees feel secure. That is the reason for the following structure.

Stages of setting the cards and 'reading' them:

1. Divide the cards into five piles, face down.

2. Think about a problem case and keep it in your mind.

3. Take five cards from any pile (or one from each pile as you wish) and hold them face down.

4. Place the cards face down according to the diagram – the top card in the middle then the next one above it, the third below them, the fourth on the left and the fifth on the right.

$$
\begin{array}{ccc}
 & 2 & \\
4 & 1 & 5 \\
 & 3 &
\end{array}
$$

5. Turn over card no.1 and ask yourself: In what way does the card represent my client's problem?

6. Turn over card nos. 2 and 3 and ask yourself: In what way are they connected to the origins (history) or causes of the problem or contribute to its understanding?

7. Card no. 4 is the hopes or fears you have for that client.

8. Card no. 5 is the issue(s) that the therapy is dealing with or that you feel need to be addressed but are maybe still in the background.

9. Please share what you have observed in the cards and discuss it with a partner. Use the cards to tell about the case and to clarify or affirm what you already know.

10. If by any chance you do not know how any one of the cards is connected to the PROBLEM, turn over the other four cards, leaving only the card you found puzzling. Free associate, tell the story of this card (not necessarily in relation to the problem) and of what you think happens with this card. Let your partner write this down, then read it back out loud to you. Ask the questions of this card once more and see if it clarifies anything. Then continue with any other card that you are stuck with, using the same process.

11. Share with your supervisor any new things that have been revealed or things that looks fascinating, or puzzling. If acceptable let the supervisor share his perception of the cards and what they may represent.

12. Now look at your cards and choose the one which says to you: 'Stop it all, there is no hope, you are useless. She (your client) is hopeless, etc.' Then choose the card which says: 'Yes, this is difficult; but you can do it; don't despair.'

13. Turn over all the other cards and stay with these two. Let them 'talk' to each other and listen to their dialog. (Let your supervisor help you in this process, by holding the card facing you, or by helping you interviewing them.) If you find any difficulty in the process then return to the full deck of cards. Divide it in the middle. Take the middle card. Look at this card. In what way can this card help you to find a solution or in what way does it clarify the difficulties or problems of the case you have chosen to bring up?

14. Repeat the process three times and point out the cards which have been most helpful or that have shed light on difficult issues.

15. If none is helpful, then your supervisor, or counterpart, may give you support and help you understand what could be the case.

16. Evaluate the process and see what are the elements you feel are helpful to a broader understanding of this case, or are useful strategic clues for future encounters with your client.

PERSONA therapeutic faces cards

The word 'persona' means:

- a mask used by an actor
- a character or personage acted, one who plays or performs any part
- a character, relation or capacity in which one acts
- a being having rights and, in later use, a human being in general.

The PERSONA cards consist of two decks of cards: 77 hand-painted color portraits depicting a wide range of people from young to old, from cultures north to south and east to west. Accompanying the portraits are 33 interaction cards that schematically indicate links and relationships. Portrait cards may be used alone or in combination with interaction cards.

When we look at these portraits, of people who could inhabit any corner of our world or of our imagination, we begin to wonder what kind of lives they live, what they feel and think, what their names are, how others see them and how they see themselves. At the same time the cards may reveal the many aspects of one person. If we select two portrait cards, we can begin to imagine a relationship with its myriad empathies and antipathies unfolding somewhere along the familiar spectrum of comedy to tragedy. An interaction card, whose significance is to be determined by the player, can help shape the fantasy and enhance the story.

Meeting the real or the phantom

PERSONA cards are very useful for clarifying the therapist's perception of the individual client, the couple, or the group. The instructions here will gradually explain how it is done with the supervisee in a consultation with a couple.

First spread all the 77 faces on the table.

1. Ask your supervisee to look at them carefully and pretend that he is the husband in this couple.

2. Ask him as the husband to choose the card representing his wife (A).

3. Then ask him to pick the card that represents him as the husband (B).

4. Now ask the supervisee to assume the role of the wife, and whilst looking at the pictures choose the picture representing her husband the way she perceives him (D), and then one to represent herself (C).

5. Ask the supervisee to pick a picture representing the man as the supervisee himself sees him, and then to pick a picture for the woman.

6. Observe together the pictures that were chosen (maximum six). Sometimes you will find out that the supervisee has picked the same picture as one of 'the couple'. Reflect on that choice. Is it the way any of them perceives himself or herself, or the way they perceive the other? Any comments on that?

7. Sometimes one member of 'the couple' chooses the same picture as his or her 'spouse'. Check with the supervisee – what does that mean?

8. Then put the supervisee's choices as in Figure 6.1.

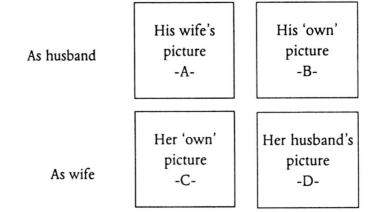

As husband

| His wife's picture -A- | His 'own' picture -B- |

As wife

| Her 'own' picture -C- | Her husband's picture -D- |

B and C – The way he assumes they perceive themselves.

A and D – Their inner perceptions of each other as the supervisee sees it.

Figure 6.1 PERSONA cards – discovering the real and the phantom

9. Ask your supervisee to tell whom does he meet in his sessions with this couple – wishes or projections on him, in short 'phantoms'. In some cases it's her 'phantom' with his 'reality' and vice versa. I think this is a very important issue in understanding how things are going on in the sessions.

10. If the way in which the supervisee sees them is different from any of them, check with him on which occasions did he meet this couple?

11. Ask the supervisee to choose from the interaction cards the arrows that represent the relationship between pictures A and B, and C and D; that is, how the supervisee sees the two as perceiving their interaction.

12. What would represent an interaction that would satisfy the supervisee as a goal for this couple?

13. What should happen in order for it to be possible?

14. Make optional dialogs between the four (or more) pictures and see where it leads.

15. Is it possible to do the same process with the couple in a session? If so, are there any preparations?

Reflect on the whole process and see what are the insights and understandings you have gained from it.

CHAPTER 7

The Spectrogram[1] – The Use of Small Objects

'It is just like chess'

Yosuf is the head of a social services department in an Arab town. Recently his team was extended and now includes a drug abuse section and an adolescent unit. Yosuf came to my supervision group saying that since these changes and developments in the team he really felt things were not as they had been. There was a lot of tension and he could see that something needed to be done. Ahmad, head of another social services department was always Yosuf's partner in our activities and they usually gave each other logical and realistic feedback. This time I thought we could use the 'small objects'. In fact I have a sample of the small objects in my bag whenever I go to give supervision, so I spread them on the table.

At first Yosuf looked surprised and said, 'Is that the best way you're going to help me – through little toys?'

'First I am not going to help you,' I answered. 'You will probably do it yourself, and perhaps Ahmad will, but I would like you to try and do this exercise to help us learn about the new space that was created in your department following these changes.'

Yosuf really wanted to go on explaining to us what had happened since the three new people arrived. So we let him describe the change from a very cohesive and dedicated group of four workers into what he called a big group of 11. I asked how this came about. Yosuf explained that the three new full-time people had an additional four people working under

---

1   Adapted from Jennings (1986)

them who are only part-time, and out of them two are freelancers who do not come to the weekly meetings.

I encouraged Yosuf to look at the table where I had sat some 40 little animals and objects and asked him to pick any of them to represent his team. Yosuf looked at the table and was quickly drawn to it. He looked at them carefully, picking them up, examining them, putting them down, and laughing. At the end he had seven pieces in front of him (see Figure 7.1). Yosuf took Miss Piggy, a shepherd, a boat, a strong lad, a rooster, the duke from The Hunchback of Notre Dame, and a snail. To start with he was asked to position them in the way that he saw them at the time.

Yosuf noticed immediately that he actually divided the group into 'old' and 'new' putting himself at a distance and the boat as a 'de facto' leader. We asked Yosuf to describe them according to their role or character. He said: 'Miss Piggy is this new lazy woman Shafi that is in charge of the rehabilitation program. She never does anything but she will always have advice and (generally negative) things to say. She is young and I feel she is stupid. The shepherd is my assistant. He comes in only three days a week the rest of the time he is at court. He is an older man, a former teacher and is very efficient.' We asked him why a shepherd? Yosuf said: 'Oh, well he is very responsible.' Next he told us that the strong lad is the new man who works with the juvenile delinquents, a very strong hard worker who hates Miss Piggy and always says "let's get rid of her". 'The boat is his deputy, a very efficient lady but always running in between. The rooster is another worker with the drug addicts who always say how wonderful they are (that is his rehab. team). The duke is the probation officer.'

This is the first time that he (Yosuf) noticed how powerful Ataf was, and he was surprised where he put him (next to Miss Piggy). He said: 'It is no coincidence, I am aware that something is going on there.' When Ahmad laughed Yosuf said: 'No romance, no...' Then to himself: 'Perhaps...' The snail was described as a very hard but slow worker: 'She is dedicated and working long hours.' But Yosuf would have liked her to move on. And for himself he chose a lion, saying: ' I have to lead, no?'

We asked him to position them the way they were before. Now the four 'original' members were very close but there was a hierarchy. Yosuf observed it and said: 'That was nice but too small and too close.'

We then asked him to position the team from each staff member's 'point of view'. Yosuf worked spontaneously and it took him at most two minutes to do this for each of them. Yosuf learnt four new things:

- that the shepherd wished to see Yosuf leave so that he could take the lead
- that the snail saw herself left out once the new team was formed
- that Miss Piggy wanted his lead but would block anyone from approaching him
- that the duke was challenging his authority at the same time as joining forces with Miss Piggy against the strong lad.

At that point we asked Yosuf to arrange the team in the way he would have liked them to be. Yosuf took some time now and then arranged them again. It was clear to him and to the group the similarity between this arrangement and that of the rooster and the snail. At the same time we noticed how far away the duke was and that the snail was between the duke and the shepherd.

Figure 7.1 Spectrogram: Talking with the duke and the shepherd

When we asked him to evaluate the process, Yosuf was quite astonished at some of the 'revelations' he had. He said, 'How wonderful this is, it is like chess, you can move one pawn and the whole situation changes.'

'Would you add or change any of these animals or objects?' I asked.

Yosuf looked and said, 'Perhaps I should add to myself this computer,' (a small computer toy that was on the table) 'the lion needs to plan and calculate his moves. This is a different group, some do not really mind the lion the way things are.'

Yosuf and Ahmad went on discussing every fine detail as they both knew all the 'actors'. Finally we asked Yosuf to try and tell us what would he do with this new perspective. His first reaction was: 'I shall ask my staff to do the same in our next staff meeting.' But after some thought said: 'Well it's hard to say right now, but perhaps I'll take this experience and have an individual talk with each member of my team. I definitely need to talk with the duke and the shepherd.'

The spectrogram, as you can see, is the use of objects – coins, pebbles, buttons, and many other objects representing whatever we wish them to represent. In some cases I have used it as a tool to help my supervisee to understand family dynamics and interrelationships together with the family's perception of the therapist: Who wants her out? Who wants her in? And where? And at times (like in the next example) to clarify the difference in the perceptions of a group by co-therapists.

Using given objects

The objects are already provided. Beads, buttons, marbles, rosettes, buckles, suspenders, etc. are all supplied in a large box or tin. If it is an individual supervision then the supervisee is asked to represent the family, client, or group using the various objects. However, when it is a group supervision, members are each given a turn to create a representation of their life, of the family, or of their role in this particular case. A record of these may be made for future use, say when trying the exercise again in three months and making comparisons.

It is extremely important to 'de-role' the objects before putting them back in the box, as a means of saying 'goodbye' to the material that came from the right hemisphere, and so returning to reality. For example, 'This fat marble was my boss but now it is a marble again.'

EXAMPLE: JOE AND LILY

One of the longest supervision groups I have been leading is a group of therapists working in a family crisis unit dealing mostly with domestic violence. Each group is led by a dramatherapist and a social worker. Joe and Lily are very experienced therapists who have been running an open group for wife batterers for the past year and a half. At this point in time they were occupied with some questions regarding the group's structure, especially as one of the group members was very aggressive and had lost control several times.

The metaphor they used was 'it is like a bus that suddenly had a flat tire.' So I asked them to build a spectrogram depicting the group (including them) handling the flat tire. I took out my basket of buttons and asked each of them to place the group as they saw it (see Figure 7.2).

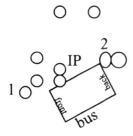

Joe's arrangement

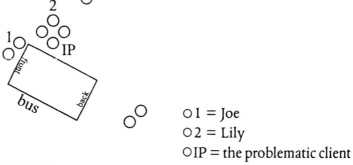

Lily's arrangement

○1 = Joe
○2 = Lily
○IP = the problematic client

Figure 7.2 Joe and Lily's bus metaphor

One can easily see that there are some aspects they see in the same way: that IP is very instrumental in this group, taking care of the flat tire; that there is someone totally outside; that there are subgroups. At the same time one can easily see how they positioned each other: whereas Lily sees Joe close to the scene; he put her far at the back.

They had many questions for each other, but most important was that they saw that they needed to work on their role perception and co-operation in the present crisis.

EXAMPLE: ME AND NOT ME ARE BOTH PARTS OF MYSELF

Sometimes I use the small objects in order to help my supervisees learn about their likes and dislikes and attractions and rejections in relation to their clients. A good example is the following session I had with Tina, a very creative art therapist who worked with battered women. On several occasions she told me that she had almost shouted at one of her battered women in her therapy group as this woman continually protected her abusive husband.

I thought that Tina would learn from the following experience and could use it with her client group too. I asked Tina to look at the shelves in my office full of small objects and to choose one that she liked and one that she disliked (that repelled her or maybe that she was just indifferent to).

Tina chose an elephant as her liked object and a bug as big as a grasshopper as her disliked object. I asked her to sit with the two objects for a while and to write down all the things that came to mind as she looked at them – any characteristics, anything about their tactile feeling, associations about them in general, or in particular to their color or shape.

Tina took some time to write, most of the time she held the elephant on her knees and put the bug on the table. When she finished I asked her to share her writing with me. She gladly read a long list confirming her original attraction and repulsion, but in two instances she said that the elephant was too fat and that the bug was quick. For her, too fat was bad and being quick was good. Otherwise the elephant was clever, caring, protective, with a very good memory, he could remember someone who 'did bad things to him and avenge after many years' (here Tina laughed). 'He is helpful, gentle and likes to be with and play with others. Although his skin is thick he is sensitive and protects others. The bug on the other hand is dirty, lives in dirt, eats dirt, bites, selfishly living on other people's blood, stupid, gets on her nerves, persistent, but in a repulsive way.' I asked Tina to imagine a place where these two can meet either in reality or in fantasy. Tina said, 'But of course, this bug is sitting on the elephant's ear and makes his terrible buzzing noise.'

'Does the elephant mind it at all?' I asked.

'Well,' she said, 'yes, but he flaps his big ears and the bug flies away.'

'Can he see him now?' I asked.

'Oh yes he is just in front of his nose.'

'And can he say anything to him?' I asked.

'Yes, he asks him why is he doing that.'

'What does the bug say?'

'He says: "I can't help it, I am a bug, I live on blood, you have good blood so I suck it!"'

'Well,' I said pretending to be the elephant, 'can't you find something else to eat?'

'Whatever I eat, people dislike me. When I eat dirt they hate it, when I eat their food they hate me. I am disliked but I don't mind it any more.'

'Was there a time that you were liked, did anyone ever like you?'

' I don't remember it but I guess my mum did.'

'And where is she now?'

'She was killed by pesticides, you know all this poison humans use against us.' She paused.

'This conversation makes me too close to this bug and I kind of feel awkward,' Tina suddenly said.

'What happened?' I asked.

'This exercise made me feel for the bug and it is funny.'

'Do you want to continue or to talk about it?'

Tina opted to talk. She said she suddenly understood why she is so frustrated with this woman. She thought that the bug is the woman's husband but then she realized it was something in that nagging person continually moaning about things, but not doing much about it. And then she said that she realized how sad she must have been and lonely, just like that bug.

'Did you notice anything about sizes?' I asked.

'You mean that I need to start a diet?'

'I am not in that business,' I said. 'I'm talking about the hugeness of the elephant and the size of the bug, and about the fact that they differ in their tempo.'

'Yes, she is kind of fast but not really, because like the bug she flies in circles. I guess she is trapped in this game.'

Then she looked at me and said, 'It reminds me of parts in me that fight all the time but I don't really feel that I identify with this woman, or do I?'

Well, you know my contract with my supervisees, so I asked Tina to decide whether she wanted to process it here, go home, reflect on it and then discuss it, or use her therapy to explore the deeper meaning of this introspection. She said she would definitely explore it in her therapy but would like to talk about it here too in relation to her role as therapist in this particular group, so we set time for that process in our next session as this one was near its end. Tina wasn't satisfied and she really wanted to have that chance now, so with the group's consent we added another 15 minutes. Tina opened a dialog with her client 'sitting' on an empty chair opposite her, she discussed her insights about the client's vulnerability and loneliness and ended up saying that she felt for her and cared about her.

Tina took the same exercise to her group some weeks later and learned so much about them and saw the women gain so much insight into their own disowned parts.

CHAPTER 8

BASIC Ph model – How to Understand the Way a Supervisee Meets the World

My main argument over the last 20 years has been that humans face a variety of challenges from day one and struggle to survive (e.g. Lahad 1995). This ongoing effort to develop in each and every one of us a unique combination of coping resources becomes the 'way we meet the world'. The basis of this ability and its development is a personal combination of genetic factors and life's learning experiences.

My principal approach is that when we meet a person who is in need of help, we should try first and foremost to perceive him as able and capable and assess not only what is wrong with that person or 'how did he fail in life', but rather try to discover what made it possible for that person to get this far. This is different from the mainstream clinical approach in psychotherapy. It takes a rather humble view of humans, looking at each of them not only as unique but also as a miracle. The miracle of survival, that we all take so easily for granted, forgetting that our 'first' days on this planet were rather difficult and not so promising, taking into account how vulnerable and helpless we were.

I believe that if we listen in a nonjudgmental, careful way to the person's language of how he describes his experience or rather of how he meets the world, we can make rapport with him, and can many a time just remind him of his abilities or broaden them (intervene). We do not attempt to change his inner structure (therapy). This may be enough.

The survival game

Historically there were several theoretical attempts to describe the human code of survival. Some of these attempts tried to present an exclusive explanation, whilst others tried to highlight one aspect in relation to previous theories. One can deduce from these attempts six fundamental elements in explaining human survival. Freud (1936) stressed the affective world, both inner (i.e. unconscious) and overt, (projection and transference) and it is Freud who stated that early emotional experiences, conflicts, and fixations determine the way a person meets the world. Often this unconscious part overrides the transactions of the real world.

His students and colleagues, Erikson (1963) and Ansbacher and Ansbacher (1956), albeit from a different angle, highlighted the role of society and the social setting in the way a person meets the world – Ansbacher and Ansbacher in their theory of inferiority and the drive for power, and Erikson in his eight stages of development.

Jung, who was originally a student of Freud, emphasized the symbolic and archetypal element, imagination, 'the culture heritage' and the fantastic inner and outer world. Jung also mentioned intuition as one of his types. Other psychological theories have dismissed the whole idea of psyche and emotion and have attempted to describe human behaviour in terms of stimulus and response. This has been called behaviorism, but we suggest that its proponents should be called 'physiologists', because their theory suggests neurochemical chains of reactions resulting in behavior (Pavlov 1927). Before long, the cognitive school found its own theory about the way a person meets the world. They phrased it 'It's all in the mind', or cognitive processes with errors of thought or perception.

Last but not least, we have the belief and meaning stream, presented by Maslow (1959) and later developed into a psychological theory and psychotherapeutic approach by Victor Frankl (1963). Based on his extreme experiences of the Holocaust he founded the Logotherapy School, which put great emphasis on the process of finding the meaning of life.

I believe that these exclusive attempts to describe human psychic life have many disadvantages and that human psychic life is more complex than the theoretical attempts to describe it on one or two dimensions. In our approach we tend to relate to the six dimensions that in our experience underlie the coping style of the client: belief and values, affect (emotional), social, imaginative, cognitive, and physiological. We have named it BASIC Ph. This multimodal approach suggests a combination between these elements in the unique coping style of each person.

Obviously, people react in more than one of these modes, and everyone has the potential to cope in all six modes, but each person develops his own special configuration. Most of us at different times have a preferred mode or modes of coping and will use this extensively. From hundreds of observations and interviews with people under stress (Lahad 1981; Shacham and Lahad 1996) it is apparent that each individual has a special way of coping and combining coping mechanisms.

In our research of coping mechanisms under stress (Lahad 1984, 1989; Shacham and Lahad 1996; Niv and Lahad 1996), we have found different coping styles. There are those whose preferred mode of coping is cognitive-behavioral. The cognitive strategies include information gathering, problem solving, self-navigation, internal conversation, or lists of activities or preferences. Another type will demonstrate an emotional or 'affective' coping mode and will use expressions of emotion (such as crying, laughter or talking with someone about their experiences); or nonverbal methods (such as drawing, reading, or writing).

A third type will opt for a social mode of coping, and receive support from belonging to a group, having a task, taking on a role, and being part of an organization. A fourth will use imagination either to mask the brutal facts (by day-dreaming, pleasant thoughts, or by diverting their attention using guided imagery) or to try to imagine additional solutions to the problem that go beyond the facts – improvisation. Type five will rely on beliefs and values to guide them through times of stress or crisis. Not only are religious beliefs meant here, political stands, beliefs, or feelings of mission (meaning) are also intended – the need for self-fulfillment and strong 'self' expressions. 'Ph'-type people are those who mainly react and cope by using physical expressions together with body movement. Their methods for coping with stress are relaxation, desensitization, physical exercise and activity. Expending energy is an important component in many modes of coping.

How can the BASIC Ph model be applied in supervision?

Based on the assumption that different people meet the world in varied ways we can identify that same approach with supervisees. When we have noticed the supervisee's style we can help her to be aware of it and use it in our supervision as a way to mediate between us. This means that at least in the beginning phase of our work, we make it our task to adapt our communications to our supervisee's channels, or we use these channels to teach our supervisee to understand why it is so difficult for her to get across to her clients and thus help her bridge the gap between them.

I feel I need to give some examples but must ask my reader to understand that for the sake of these examples I have to use generalizations and stereotypes.

Sometimes we meet a supervisee who is very detached, using logic and abstract concepts, quoting research and rules, and insisting on every fine detail. We may find that sort of person rather aggravating but let's look at it from the BASIC Ph perspective. This person is using mostly C and perhaps some B. Another type of supervisee is very intuitive, uses images and metaphors, much emotional and affective descriptions, and it is rather difficult to get a straight answer and hard facts from him. It may be that the main channels for that person are A and I. The judgmental supervisee is the one who puts values to his actions, seeing them in a rather philosophical manner or sometimes in black and white. He is the B type supervisee who at times seems incapable of compromise. The 'hyperactive', always busy supervisee incorporates some Ph aspects in his approach to life.

As can be seen in Figure 8.1, we call the interaction/ meeting between ME and WORLD the BASIC Ph exchange space. That is the area where the individual meets the world. The area that does not meet the world is all those 'languages' that for some reason the person does not use, but potentially will be able to use. That's why we call them 'forgotten' rather than unknown. The potential for smooth communication and understanding between supervisor and supervisee is in this exchange space. However, if it is not possible to bridge over, it is preferable to move into the 'forgotten' language. This involves changing the contract to one of a therapeutic nature.

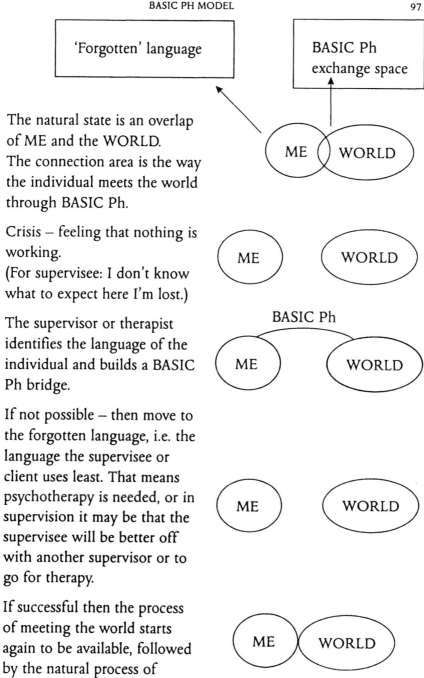

The natural state is an overlap of ME and the WORLD.
The connection area is the way the individual meets the world through BASIC Ph.

Crisis – feeling that nothing is working.
(For supervisee: I don't know what to expect here I'm lost.)

The supervisor or therapist identifies the language of the individual and builds a BASIC Ph bridge.

If not possible – then move to the forgotten language, i.e. the language the supervisee or client uses least. That means psychotherapy is needed, or in supervision it may be that the supervisee will be better off with another supervisor or to go for therapy.

If successful then the process of meeting the world starts again to be available, followed by the natural process of overlap.

Figure 8.1 The negotiation with the world according to the BASIC Ph model

It is quite possible to listen to the 'story' that your supervisee tells you in the first meeting or at any other stage and while actively listening to the story to assess the way it is told, that is the BASIC Ph components. This is the basis for the interaction we have developed. Interaction is an outcome of the location of coping resources and is a basis for an open dialog and mutual assessment of its validity.

For example, in one case the supervisee and I identified that his client's language of coping was more in the B mode, beliefs and values, and his main resources were techniques related to values clarification. We then assumed that the most appropriate forms of intervention for this person would be activities encouraging the search for meaning such as logotherapy, or techniques of value clarification and orders of preference. That is what is meant by attempting to meet him in his own space.

In a hypothetical case, where the assessment showed the following configurations, S (social), C (cognitive), and I (imaginative), we can offer the following suggestions. In the cognitive mode they include, primarily, information gathering and problem solving. Since the person has been shown to have imaginative capabilities, ordinary problem solving is not enough for him, but improvisation and the ability to imagine solutions over and beyond the routine solution may well be. This means developing resourcefulness and the ability to find alternative solutions, or in the words of Watzlawick, Weakland and Fisch (1979), 'second degree solutions'. In addition, since we are talking about someone in whom social facets of coping have been identified, solutions in the problem-solving exercise can be directed towards social targets such as taking on a new role or responsibility in a group or organization.

Experience taught me that within a relatively short time one can learn to plan an initial intervention programme from which either a longer-term treatment program will come about or a short intervention will suffice.

Six-part story making

One structured way to assess the coping resources and the language of the client is six-part story making (6-PSM) (Lahad 1992b), where we ask the client to tell us a story according to six questions. The six answers to these questions are either drawn in a cartoon style (see Figure 8.2) or are told or written as a story. The six questions are:

- Who is the main character of the story (real, imaginative, single, few, human, animal, hero or heroine)?
- What is the task or mission of that character?
- Who or what can help in this task (if at all)?
- What is the obstacle in the way? What prevents it from happening?
- How does the main character go about it? How does he cope with the obstacle?
- What is the outcome? The end? Or any possible continuity?

When the client tells his story the therapist must listen to it on several levels:

- the tone in which the story is told
- the context of the story and its message (themes)
- finding the dominant coping modes of the story (BASIC Ph).

Why do we ask these questions? Von Franz (1987), the great researcher of fairy tales and stories from a Jungian approach, has found that these six elements are always represented in fairy tales the world round. She quoted Jung as saying that 'It is in fairy tales that one can best study the comparative anatomy of the psyche' (p. 11), and that the basic and maybe only archetype is that of the self reflected in many ways. Von Franz herself says that fairy tales are the purest and simplest expression of collective, unconscious psychic processes (p. 1). Later she states: 'Personally, I think that the most frequent way archetypal stories originate is through individual experiences.' (p. 16.)

Our assumption is that by telling a projected story based on elements of fairy tale and myth, we may be able to see the way that the self projects itself in organized reality in order to meet the world.

Each picture gives us information on coping modes. If, for example, the hero is of the fairy world, that gives a suggestion or hints at the use of imagination. The goal can be connected with values and beliefs. The help can be practical or imaginary, or maybe an inner belief. The obstacle can be social, imaginary, or very realistic and demanding of a solution. Coping can come in all kinds of ways and the conclusion can be emotional, intellectual, social, or imaginary. Therefore it is important to pay attention and to determine the modes the individual does and does not utilize, and to begin the contact according to those lines.

The way in which we analyze the most developed coping modes is by counting the number of times each mode appeared; the coping mode most frequently mentioned is the one most used. The following examples are quoted verbatim and may appear somewhat confusing. The example, below, of 6-PSM is from a child aged 9. He was referred because of social problems on a background of difficult parent–child relations. (In brackets appear the BASIC Ph modes. See Table 8.1 for a full explanation of BASIC Ph symbols and their interpretations.)

- Once upon a time there was a flower (C) and it was small (Ph).

- When it grew up (Ph) its mission was to get to another flower (S).

- He had an assistant (S, Ph) who raised him and he had a bow and arrow (C, I).

- The obstacles were a man (S-) with a gun and fire (Ph) which surrounded the flower.

- The man who looked after the flower (S) shot (Ph) the man (S-) with the gun and he also had a hose pipe (C), so the flower managed to get to the other flower (S).

- In the end the good man (A) brought the two (Ph) flowers to his garden (C). I've also drawn his footsteps. (See Figure 8.2)

Analyzing his story according to BASIC Ph has led to the following: 4C, 6Ph, I, 4S, 2S-, A. In order to clarify some parts we 'interview' the story. The interview took the following lines:

Q: Why did he decide that he wanted to go to the other flower?

A: Because he didn't want to be alone, it was the only flower. Around him was desert, at first he thought that the grass was his friend, but when he grew up he noticed that he was different and alone. When they were fighting also the grass grew and this helped him, I mean that the grass can also help the man against the desert, but he still wants someone like him.

Q: What did the flowers say to him?

A: They said that they had waited a long time for him and it was boring without him. The flowers will be friends.

Q: What will happen if they separate?

A: If they separate then he will feel sad, but then he'll go and look for another flower, but not in this area.

Table 8.1 Major configurations of BASIC Ph and their interpretations

B   Self-reliant, clear values, views and beliefs

BC   Very rigid or concrete beliefs and opinions

BA   Very sensitive beliefs and opinions, sometimes some imaginary beliefs

BS   Social values

A   Affect of all types

A-   Aggressive feeling against the self and general destruction

AS   Social emotion, (similar to BS) or social support

AI   Emotions mixed with imaginary characters, frightening dragons, monsters, etc.

AC   An inclination to understand emotions by conceptualization, occasionally also neutralization or control of emotion by intellect

S   Social, inclination to take a task upon oneself, to be in need of company, not necessarily for support but for a sense of purpose – a source of support in the social setting and in organizations

SC   Socially aware and capable of solving problems, practical under conditions of stress

SI   Social support from imaginary figures such as Superman

S-   Feeling of alienation or rejection by society, hostility

I   Broad imagination either in content or range

IC   Improvisational ability based on factual knowledge

I-   Morbid imagination

C   Cognition, knowledge, organization and thought, acting according to common sense with concrete tasks

CPh   Concrete ways of thinking, action-oriented

C-   Apparent reason for activity but without logic (e.g. going to the seaside because it's winter), lack of reality testing

Ph   Physical, very physically expressive, full of activity – movement, eating, suffering, dancing, travelling, etc.

Ph-   Psychosomatic ailments or wish to commit suicide

Note – Whenever the minus sign appears it signifies a conflict in that particular category. It refers to a coping resource that due to existing circumstances reflects the distress of the individual.

Figure 8.2 The six-part story

There are other uses for the six-part story, such as use of the story content itself. We will not expand here on these uses of the story, but will merely mention that by looking at the themes, subjects, conflicts, and deliberations of the hero, one can check the stance and current emotional state of the storyteller. All this can be done on an interpretative or an analytical level, dynamically or with a gestalt approach to allow the storyteller to identify with different parts of the story and thus clarify the special meaning of the story for the storyteller himself here and now.

CHAPTER 9

Supervising Crisis Intervention Teams

Over the past 15 years I have been engaged with a number of crisis and disaster intervention teams who were working with the victims in the aftermath of terrorist attacks. One of the risks these teams face is that by being in such close proximity to the site and in such proximity with human suffering they themselves may develop ASR (acute stress reactions) or even PTSD (post-traumatic stress disorder). (Lahad 1999a, 1999b.) This phenomenon was called by Figley (1995) 'compassion fatigue'.

The usual way of working with rescue forces or psychosocial crisis intervention teams is with a structured reality oriented method called CISD (critical incident stress debriefing). (Mitchell 1983.) However, as some of the groups are exposed to recurrent disasters they may need further assistance, still in the format of group supervision, that maintains some of the professional façade and yet allows closeness to the emotional load they carry with them. Therefore I found the use of the dramatic distancing offered by creative supervision to encompass these qualities. In dramatic distancing we mean enabling the supervisees to look at the event from the protective distance a projected role gives.

EXAMPLE: ALL THE KING'S HORSES AND ALL THE KING'S MEN

I met these nine helpers a few days after they had been involved in a disaster. This was their third incident in the past five months. All of them had been through CISD sessions, but the group showed signs of fatalism, tiredness, and apathy. Some were in constant contact with individuals and families of previous disasters, despite the fact that it was not their official role. Some were manifesting anger and discomfort, but all were very dedicated to their role as helpers and continued to report at any incident. I was offered three sessions of crisis supervision with them.

The atmosphere at the start of our meeting was a combination of 'He (me, the supervisor) will solve all our problems' and 'What can really be done? – It is a hopeless situation.' I immediately registered in my head the parallel processes between them and their clients moving on the scale between despair and omnipotence.

I decided to start with movement (as they had talked enough through the CISD sessions). I put on the different sides of the room the words: Hope, Despair, Fear, and Courage. The instructions were to move around the room and whenever they got near the signs either to stop or reflect, to write or draw anything, or make a movement or a sound.

I then asked each of them to choose one of the corners and meet the other members that chose the same place. (If anyone found it difficult to choose a place he or she was encouraged to find a position between the two signs depicting the feeling at that moment.) Everyone found a corner except one who positioned himself between 'Courage' and 'Despair'.

The next step was to communicate for about five minutes without words but with signs, sounds, and movements the feelings, thoughts and sensations that this corner brought up. They were then to share two to four sentences each, making a joint poem or prose and to stage it as a choir. They could decide on the rhythm and tempo or they could use a known melody. This took about half an hour. Then, they were asked to perform the outcome and the listeners/observers were asked to write down anything that came to mind or any image or sentence they liked from that performance. The mood in the group shifted to the Ph, S, and I modes, that is physical, social, and imaginative, but still many tears were shed even at this stage (A).

When they were asked to share what happened some said that the poems and moreover, the melody or rhythm put them in touch with their impotence. Dark, darkness, and dark colors were very apparent in the images and words. A few members were in tears talking about the permission to grieve. Some said that the poems they wrote, and more than that the time they were by themselves but still with others, gave them for the first time permission to express sorrow and grief publicly. The helper who was between the two signs talked about impotence and inability to choose, he cried and laughed at the same time and when asked to describe that he said: 'Crying is about my own losses in life, laughing is the relief to be able to share that without fear.'

The next supervision session was opened by reading Humpty Dumpty. They all knew it, but did not connect it to their experience. The purpose of bringing the verse (a distancing technique) was to look into their need to put all the pieces together, how frustrating and impossible a task this was, and to allow the expression of their anger towards the 'king' who in their minds expected them to put Humpty together again.

They were now encouraged to take different roles and experiment with different inner and outer dialogs. For most of them it was the first time they realized the impossible role they were putting themselves in, the need to fix things for others, their fantasy of replacing the irreplaceable and the enormous pressure this puts on them. The 'king' was demystified and there followed heavy attacks and expressions of anger and frustrations toward the 'king' who expects so much of them. The last part of the session was a guided imagery leading to a meeting with Humpty Dumpty and sharing with him 'what I can and what I can't do for him'. Sharing these thoughts in the form of a letter was the end of the session.

The third supervision session was dedicated to re-entry. That is, to sharing of skills or activities they do in order to reduce symptoms, uncomfortable feelings, or other distressing issues. We put a huge basket in the middle of the room and asked each one to write on a separate piece of paper one thing that was still distressful. Each one could put as many papers in the basket as they wanted. Then I asked them to take a paper randomly from the basket and react to it, passing it then to the next person to add ideas. If anyone took out their own paper they could either respond to it or put it back. However, once the paper they had drawn was returned to them, they kept it. This was a very busy session, but at the end many of the 'problems' got some ideas and answers, some in the form of cognitive advice, others with practical ideas, and some 'just' with words of comfort and support.

Finally, the participants were encouraged to either keep the 'answer' or 'throw it out, get rid of it' by symbolically throwing it to the garbage or destroying it and saying goodbye to it. Only three out of the nine participants went for the second option. We concluded the session by talking about compassion fatigue and how to prevent it. Training the participants in self-relaxation ended the session.

CHAPTER 10

Resistance – Or Waiting in the Hallway

Resistance, one of the common aspects of encounter with people, causes much distress to many therapists and supervisors. In fact I have found that resistance brings up for many helpers feelings of failure, desertion, betrayal accompanied by anger, self-doubt, resentment, and overambition. Perhaps this is more so for younger supervisors and therapists, who see it as a threat to their ability to bridge over to anyone.

Coming from an existential theory and influenced by gestalt approach, I found it a very important aspect of my encounter with my supervisees. This voice inside may say to me 'stop being so deaf, listen to me', it may say ' I am on my own now, let me grow'; yet it could mean ' I am at the hallway, there are many doors ahead some look rather frightening, don't push me, let me explore the doors, the handles, before I am getting into it', it could mean so many things but I will try as much as possible not to get into the 'blaming game'.

So as I listen to the sounds inside, I may say: 'Welcome, there is a possibility or a potential here we just need "TIME and PATIENCE"', as old General Kutuzov says in *War and Peace*.

Games of supervision

Rabinovitz (1995) highlights the interplay between supervisors and supervisees calling them 'games of supervision'. She identifies a kind of a dance both supervisees and supervisors dance and how the one's dance influences the other's reactions. She defines six types of games: 'control and standards', 'redefinition of supervisory relationship', 'reducing the power gap', 'transfer of control to the supervisee', 'giving-up games', 'power games'. Let me give some examples of these games, as I believe awareness of these games can be one way of working through. We will start with the games supervisees play but do remember 'it takes two to tango'.

Games supervisees play

CONTROL AND STANDARDS

Name of the game: *'Be nice to me and I'll be nice to you'* – flattering the supervisor.

Supervisee's gains: Helps the supervisee to control standards through emotional blackmail so that the supervisor will find it hard to ask for standards.

Why supervisor gets into the game: Feelings of satisfaction as a model figure.

REDEFINING SUPERVISION RELATIONSHIP

Name of the game: *'Take care of me, don't punch me'* – the supervisee prefers to expose himself rather than his work.

Supervisee's gains: The move from a supervisory to a client–therapist relationship reduces demands from the supervisor and diverts attention to personal issues.

Why supervisor gets into the game: 'I like being a therapist, I am intrigued, flattered.'

Name of the game: *'Friends do not evaluate each other'* – the supervisee tries to stress the friendly part rather than the formal aspect.

Supervisee's gains: As a friend the supervisor will not be able to evaluate my work.

Why supervisor gets into the game: 'I don't like to be perceived as an autocratic figure.'

REDUCING POWER GAPS

Name of the game: 'If you knew Dostoevski the way I do' – maneuvering the supervisor to areas he knows little or nothing about.

Supervisee's gains: Reducing power and anxiety.

Why supervisor gets into the game: Feels attacked but does not want to expose his weakness.

Name of the game: 'Well, what do you know about this?' – supervisee refers to his advantage in knowledge or experience.

Supervisee's gains: Reducing the power gap and anxiety.

Why supervisor gets into the game: Feels attacked but does not want to expose his weakness.

Name of the game: 'Frankly my dear, I don't give a damn'. – supervisee uses obscene words especially when he feels it is unpleasant to the supervisor.

Supervisee's gains: Shocking the supervisor and undermining his power.

Why supervisor gets into the game: 'I don't want to be seen as conservative.' Transferring control to supervisee.

Name of the game: 'I am shattered' – supervisee claims that he is broken-hearted and may collapse if pushed any further.

Supervisee's gains: Avoidance of sensitive issues.

Why supervisor gets into the game: 'I will not press as he is in such a delicate condition.'

Name of the game: 'I did what you told me' – supervisee shifts responsibility for the case to the supervisor, saying he is only following directives.

Supervisee's gains: Turning the all-powerful supervisor into a defensive one.

Why supervisor gets into the game: 'I am responsible, this is my chance to show him how to handle things. I like parent–child relations.'

Name of the game: 'It is all so confusing' – supervisee brings other authorities' approaches to the same problem and feels confused.

Supervisee's gains: Supervisor will be on the defensive, he will have to compete with anonymous approach and he is less of an authority.

Why supervisor gets into the game: Doesn't want to be seen as someone who can't defend his strategies.

Games supervisors play

GIVING-UP GAMES

Name of the game: 'I was wondering why you said that'.

Supervisor's gains: 'All the responsibilities for explanations are on the supervisee. I can relax and maintain my position.'

Why supervisee gets into the game: Afraid to lose face; in defense of his professionalism.

Name of the game: 'I can hardly breathe'.

Supervisor's gains: Defense against supervision. No need to take things too seriously.

Why supervisee gets into the game: No need to work hard, no criticism, no need to expose his work.

POWER GAMES

Name of the game: 'Father and mother know better'.

Supervisor's gains: Establishing his superiority on seniority and experience that are beyond questioning, and not on knowledge.

Why supervisee gets into the game: Fear for his position, and feeling vulnerable.

Name of the game: 'I am only trying to help' (I know you can't do it without me).

Supervisor's gains: Control disguised as help. Supervisor never becomes tainted, as the supervisee did not follow his suggestions.

Why supervisee gets into the game. Fear for his position, and feeling vulnerable.

The inner dialog

We have already discussed self-correspondence techniques, or inner dialogs as we called them in chapter 4. We believe they can be very useful techniques in helping supervisees to air their views openly. These may sometimes serve as an inner preparatory step aiming at clarifying relations between supervisor and supervisee and may be useful when facing resistance or other obstacles on the way to find grounding. The following is just one example of the use of such techniques to overcome resistance.

EXAMPLE: STANDING IN THE HALLWAY OR 'ENJOY THE CURRENTS'

Ab was a new supervisee who had come from the United States a few months before. Despite the fact that he was a qualified educational psychologist there, the authorities in Israel demanded a period of supervision before endorsing his license.

It was rather clear that Ab saw himself as very experienced and that supervision reminded him all the time of his difficulties as a newcomer and the loss of status he underwent. We opened up that issue rather early on and I asked him to tell me why he opted for creative supervision. His answer was that as he knew little about creative work he thought that might be a good opportunity to learn something new, and he added that he thought it would make it easier for him to accept supervision.

Life with Ab wasn't that easy; he played many of the games, but most of all 'Well, what do you know about this?' and 'I tried your ideas and they didn't work'. He was also a very cognitively oriented psychologist and, I dare say, person. Creative games didn't really appeal to him.

One day, after another trick of 'fighting' me as the representative of all those in his workplace that did not recognize his abilities, I said to him that I felt rather sad that he was stuck in this corridor with so many doors, all seemed locked but actually some were only closed. Ab gave me one of his sharp looks and said: 'What do you mean, closed locked?'

Instead of getting into conversation I said: 'Do you really want to know?' He nodded his head and I added: 'It is a process of guided fantasy, do you really want it?'

Ab agreed and I asked him to get into some form of relaxation that he knew. I then asked him to imagine a very impressive house or building in any style he wanted...

There is an inscription on the top but you find it hard to read from where you are as it is very high up and the sun is very bright though you may have a glimpse of it.

As you walk in you see a very long corridor or a hallway and many many doors all closed. At the side of each door is a sign with a word written on it. Some of the doors are locked some are just closed and at first glance you can't tell which is which. The light in the corridor is bright but can be dimmed, the walls can be decorated or left clear, the doors can be made of any material.

Then, if you observe them closely, that is if you really study them carefully, you will be able to find those that are only closed. But what does 'observe them closely' mean?

Well, that means patience, studying every detail of the door, handle, door seals, hinges and so on but even more so, with intuition.

Look at the doors and find the one that you wish to open, look at the ones you wish to be locked, look at the ones you are indifferent to, and position yourself in front of the one you wish to concentrate on.

The door that draws your attention may be the one that is connected to the inscription on the building, or to anything else.

It took a while for Ab to nod his head, indicating that he had found the door, then I said to him just to observe it and see whether it will be a locked or a closed one. And even then to not attempt to open it yet. Ab looked very relaxed and the only thing that disclosed any excitement were his eyebrows, as if he was observing something carefully. I told Ab that he could open his eyes at any time, try any of the handles, or just look or leave that corridor altogether. The only thing that maybe would be clearer to him at the end would be the inscription on the wall. 'When you open your eyes you may draw what you have seen or write it down.'

Ab opened his eyes and started writing. He wrote for more than 20 minutes and it was all to do with the experience of watching all the doors. When he finished he read it to me, and he told me that the inscription wasn't very clear but he knew what it meant – 'enjoy the currents'. Here was the door that suddenly opened for him. It wasn't the door he intended to open (for that one he knew very well) but the one with a light coming from underneath it; and as he looked at it, it opened wide. Ab continued to talk in metaphors, colors, and images as I had never heard him before, and just before he finished he looked at me with one of his grim looks and said: 'Closed doors are not less frightening than locked ones, only if you touch their handle they open up.' Then to my surprise he said: 'I guess I am learning how to take risks, no, I guess I'm learning how to enjoy the currents.'

'The wall' technique (chapter 5) and many other methods mentioned in various other chapters can also serve as a key or compass for exploration of, and working through, resistance.

Self-supervision

It so happens that even the luckiest ones can never get supervision for every client they have. But the sad reality is that many therapists are going along with very little, if any, supervision. This issue becomes even more complicated when we are talking about senior staff. They find it very difficult to get supervision in their workplace, and many times they make decisions without anyone to consult with.

I believe that the techniques described in this chapter can be very helpful for self-supervision. I have used them myself when I was involved in crisis intervention far away from home and had to look into the situation and my own involvement in order to be able to continue my support for the victims with whom I was working. The process is somewhat exhausting to start with but as you get more skilled and proficient, it works beautifully.

We all have an inner representation of the 'client', the 'therapist', and the 'supervisor'. These inner representations are present in every instance when we are facing our clients. At times it is the inner client that reacts to the situation and at other times it is the therapist that takes the lead, and then again it may be the supervisor that influences everything. However, we are not always aware which of them is active, who is making a coalition with whom, who is manipulating whom, and so on.

Step I

The first step is to take three separate pages and write on the first CLIENT, on the second THERAPIST, and on the third SUPERVISOR. Then choose a color that represents that part. On the appropriate paper draw a shape or image with that color. When you have finished drawing all the three then move to the next step.

Note. If you really feel that you need more than one color to represent a part take another one but try not to go above two colors.

Step II

Look at each of your images separately and write down all the associations you have to the color or image that you made. Then look at your color and try to imagine all the characteristics you see in it. Ask yourself if this color reminds you of someone's name or even any name. Then ask yourself what is the gender of this color. Look into your list and answers and see if you have any questions. If you have a question write it with your dominant hand and the answer with your non-dominant hand. For example, if the name that you got was Richard and the gender was female. Write the question with your right hand: 'How come you are Richard and a female?' Then take the pen in your non-dominant hand and answer it. It is preferable that you use that same color as the image for writing the answer.

Sometimes the answer may be puzzling, do not hesitate to write another question and check it. Using the non-dominant hand for writing the answer is believed by some to help get a direct answer or link to the unconscious mind. List all the typical sentences or statements that this role may use.

From now on you call each of them either by a dominant trait like 'smarty' or 'whiney' or by the name that came up for them like 'Richard', and not 'client', 'therapist', or 'supervisor'.

Step III

Now ask each part what does it think or feel about the other two. Write the answer with your non-dominant hand. If you have questions repeat the process as before.

You may find that some of the answers surprise you, do ask about it until you feel you have got an answer. If you find that any part is using other parts' sentences do ask that part about it.

Step IV

Ask each part whether it will agree to meet the other parts to discuss an urgent issue that you are concerned about. Tell them you want to invite them for coffee. Listen to their answers. If you sense any objection, go on asking why.

Step V

Write down the problem you wish to discuss as a question, such as 'Am I getting too close to this client?' Let each part answer. Listen carefully and check whether any one disguises itself as another part using its words or sentences. Continue this dialog between the parts posing questions and answering on behalf of the different parts using the non-dominant hand technique.

Step VI

Evaluate what you got from this dialog. Reflect on the process and see where it took you. Did you notice coalitions? Opposition? Self-deception? Perhaps it only clarified some of the confusion, perhaps it led you to see a new direction.

In any case from now on, you can use this technique to self-supervise whenever you wish. You will only need a notebook and to remember the name of the parts. I found the first time tiring but thereafter quite astonishing in its ability to supervise oneself when there is no supervisor available.

CHAPTER 12

Beginnings and Endings

How do we know it's time to end? Campbell (1988) says:

> I can give you example from what I know of students in arts studios. There
> comes a time when they have learned what the artist can teach them. They
> have assimilated the craft, and they are ready for their own flight. Some of
> the artists allow their students to do that. They expect the student to fly
> off. Others want to establish a school, and the student finds he has got to
> be nasty to the teacher, or to say things about him, in order to get his own
> flight. But that is the teacher's own fault. He ought to have known it was
> time for the student to fly. The students I know, the ones who are really
> valid as students, know when it is time to push off...there is an old prayer
> that says: Lord, teach us when to let go... (pp.154–155)

One day a supervisee asked me: 'And what is maturity for a therapist?' I
had several responses: the first was when you will admit that as much as
your client needs you, you need your client, but that you don't allow that
need to take the foreground, only the background. This was a clever
'parenting' answer. And then I said: 'You see, in nature there are two kinds
of maturing. One is a process that ends in decay, like with fruits – an apple
for example will rot if left on a shelf or on the tree. But you see,' I added,
'there is the other maturing that is making things better and better, like
fermenting in wine. Well, beware of the decay and try to maintain your
fermenting elements. Age and experience are beneficial as long as we do
not forget to play and be alive. After all, creativity is the flame of life.'

A Maori creation myth I once heard from my late friend Mara Capi, a therapist and healer, tells us that in the beginning heaven and earth were together, and in the space between the breast of heaven and the breast of earth there lived the gods, their offspring. It was dark there and as they multiplied it was crowded too. So the gods and sons of gods wanted to get out. God of the rivers pushed with his legs, god of the mountains pushed with his hands, god of the trees lay on his back and pushed and pushed. But nothing moved, and the god of the wind was compassionate.

And so in the space between the breast of heaven and the breast of earth lived all gods and sons of gods and they multiplied and wanted to get out.

So again God of the rivers pushed with his legs, god of the mountains pushed with his hands, god of the trees lay on his back and pushed and pushed. But nothing moved, and the god of the wind was compassionate.

But then the god of the rivers and the god of the trees pushed harder and harder until a tiny light shone in. And heaven and earth started to go apart, and a cry from one end of the world to the other was heard: 'Why are you doing that to us? Why are you pushing us apart?'

And heaven went up to the sky and earth remained beneath. Since then earth is feeding the offspring of the gods and heaven watches and protects them from up high.

Relaxation – finale

It is very helpful, in my mind, to assist the supervisee to visualize the end of therapy or the encounter with the supervisor as the end of a process. The following are examples of such ways of assisting with that ritualization.

Invite the supervisee to sit comfortably with eyes closed. She should imagine she has just been in a theater watching a play in which she has also participated. The play has not ended but has come to a temporary pause. It is the right time to reflect on the play – the most significant scene(s), a meaningful actor or actress, the director, and more. Then I say: 'Now, visualize the tableau at the end of the play, with the curtain slowly falling, and let all the pictures, sounds, and movements ebb away slowly sinking into the memory. Gradually the lights come up and you will find yourself back in the here and now. Now, open your eyes and stretch out to mark the end of the exercise.'

Let the supervisee share how was the play and the parting from that interesting and perhaps meaningful experience.

At times I'll ask my supervisees each to choose three cards out of the SAGA card game without looking at them. I then say: 'Now put them in a row facing down. Open them from left to right. The first is how you came to this supervision, the second card is what happened to you during this supervision (the positive and negative things), and the last is where you go from here.'

They may start by looking at each other's cards and giving each other feedback. Or else I let each of them look at his own cards and tell his story.

It is time to say goodbye, it is time when the offspring are strong enough to find their own way and for the supervisor to say: 'I am here, but you go your own way.' And so, perhaps it is time for a last Hasidic story.

When Rabbi Zussia was very old and was so weak he could not get out of bed, he knew that his days were few. He called his beloved students to his bedside and told them in a very soft but clear voice: 'All my life I tried to be as righteous as Moses, as holy as his brother Aaron the high priest, as clever as Joseph, and as wise as King Solomon. And now that my days are few and soon I will be called upon the highest court in front of the Lord and all the angels they will ask me to defend myself.' The old man sighed and then continued: 'Standing there I will have to tell them about my life, but they will not be interested to know how was I as Moses, Aaron, King

David, or King Solomon. All they will be asking me is, how was I as Rabbi Zussia.'

So not only let them go their own way but wish them to be themselves.

References

Ansbacher, H.L and Ansbacher, R.R. (eds) (1956) *The Individual Psychology of Alfred Adler*. New York: Basic Books.

Ande, M. (undated) *The Never Ending Story*. Stuttgart: Thienemanns Verlag.

Ankori, M. (1989) *This Forest has No End*. Tel-Aviv: Gebel Publishers.

Ayalon, O. (1997) 'Helping the Helper.' *Booklet for Seminar in Croatia*.

Bergman, Z. and Witztum, E. (1987) 'Letters to meaningful others: a psychotherapeutic tool.' *Sichot 1*, 2 112–122.

Bernard, J. and Goodyear, R. (1993) *Fundamentals of Clinical Supervision*. Boston: Allyn and Bacon.

Campbell, J. (1988) *The Power of Myth*. New York: Doubleday.

Cohen, A. (1995) *Writing Your Life – Self-Therapy Through Writing*. Tel-Aviv: Amatzia Publishers.

de Saint-Exupéry, A. (1982) *The Little Prince*. London: Pan Books.

de Shazer, S. (1985) *Keys to Solution in Brief Therapy*. New York: W.W. Norton and Company.

Ekstein, R. and Wallerstein, R.S. (1972) *The Teaching and Learning of Psychotherapy*. New York: Basic Books.

Erikson, E.H. (1963) *Childhood and Society*. New York: Norton.

Figley, Ch. (1995) (ed) *Compassion Fatigue*. New York: Brunner/Mazel.

Frankl, V. (1963) *Man's Search for Meaning*. Boston: Beacon Press.

Freud, Z. (1936) *Inhibition Symptoms and Anxiety*. London: Hogarth Press.

Hawkins, P. and Shohat, R. (1989) *Supervision in the Helping Profession. An Individual, Group and Organizational Approach*. Buckingham: Open University Press.

Jennings, S. (1986) *Creative Drama and Groupwork*. Bicester: Winslow Press.

Kadushin, A. (1992) *Supervision in Social Work*. Columbia University Press.

Kubobi, D. (1987) 'Consultation and guidance of educators based on literary texts.' In N. Reichman (ed) *Supervision*. Jerusalem: The Hebrew University Publishers.

Lahad, S. (1984) 'Evaluation of multi modal programme to strengthen coping in children and teachers under stress of shelling.' *Ph.D. dissertation*. California: Columbia Pacific University.

Lahad, M. and Cohen, A. (eds) (1989) *Community Stress Prevention Vol. 1*. Community Stress Prevention Center, Kiryat Shmona.

Lahad, M. and Cohen, A. (eds) (1992a) *Community Stress Prevention Vol. 2.* Community Stress Prevention Center, Kiryat Shmona.

Lahad, M. (1992b) 'Story-making in assessment method for coping with stress: six-piece story making and BASIC Ph.' In S. Jennings (ed) *Dramatherapy Theory and Practice 2.* London: Routledge.

Lahad, M. (1995) 'Masking the gas mask: brief intervention using metaphor, imagery, movement and enactment.' In A. Gersie (ed) *Dramatic Approaches to Brief Therapy.* London: Jessica Kingsley Publishers.

Lahad, M. (1999a) 'Supervision of crisis intervention teams: The myth of the savior.' In E. Tselikas-Portmann (ed) *Supervision and Dramatherapy.* London: Jessica Kingsley Publishers.

Lahad, M. (1999b) 'The use of drama therapy with crisis intervention groups, following mass evacuation.' *The Arts in Psychotherapy 26,* 1, 27–33.

Maslow, A.H. (1959) 'Cognition of being in the peak experiences.' *Journal of Genetic Psychology 94,* 43–66.

Minuchin, S. (1974) *Families and Family Therapy.* Cambridge, MA: Harvard University Press.

Mills, J.C. and Crowley, R.J. (1986) *Therapeutic Metaphors for Children and The Child Within.* New York: Brunner Mazel Publishers.

Mitchell, J. (1983) 'When disaster strikes…the critical incident stress debriefing process.' *Journal of Emergency Medical Services 8,* 36–39.

Niv, S. and Lahad, M. (1996) 'The Influence of a Psycho-educational Preventive Program on Children's Coping with Recurrent Traumatic Events.' *Ph.D. dissertation.* Utah: Newport University.

Oaklander, V. (1970) *Windows to Our Children.* Utah: Real People Press.

Pavlov, I.P. (1927) *Condition Reflex: An Investigation of the Physiological Activity of the Central Cortex.* London: Oxford University Press.

Rabinovitz, R. (1995) 'Connected vessels – supervision in social work theory, process and tools.' In J. Zilberman (ed) *Supervision in Social Work.* Tel-Aviv: Central School of Social Workers.

Shacham, Y. and Lahad, M. (1996) 'Stress Reaction and Activation Coping Resources: A Comparison between Children who Remained under Katyusha Shelling and Children who were Evacuated to a Safe Haven.' *Ph.D. dissertation.* Utah: Newport University.

von Franz, M.L. (1987) *Interpretation of Fairytales.* Dallas: Spring Publishers.

Watzlawick, P., Weakland, R. and Fisch, R. (1979) *Change, Principles of Problem Formation and Problem Resolution.* Palo Alto: Mental Research Institute.

Subject Index

Author Index

Lightning Source UK Ltd.
Milton Keynes UK
17 December 2009

147680UK00001B/89/P